30-MINUTE COOKING FOR ONE

30-Minute Cooking for One

85 NO-WASTE RECIPES MADE EASY

Amelia Levin

ROCKRIDGE
PRESS

Interior and Cover Designer: John Clifford
Art Producer: Sara Feinstein
Editor: Gurvinder Singh Gandu

Photography © 2021 Elysa Weitala, cover; Emulsion Studio, p. ii; Stocksy/Jeff Wasserman, p. vi; Darren Muir, p. x; Stocksy/Tara Nicole, p. 14; Hélène Dujardin, p. 28, 94; Stocksy/Nataša Mandić, p. 44; Stocksy/Ina Peters, p. 60; Stocksy/Davide Illini, p. 76; Shutterstock.com, p. 112; Stocksy/Danil Nevsky, p. 122. Food styling by Victoria Woollard, cover.

ISBN: Print 978-1-64876-707-4 | eBook 978-1-64876-708-1
R0

Dedicated to all
my solo cook friends
who provided me with
a wealth of ideas
for the book.

CONTENTS

INTRODUCTION

I get it. Cooking for one is hard. But it doesn't have to be.

Allow me to rephrase. The "motivation" to cook for one can be hard. Why bother dirtying dishes and going through the effort of creating a meal when it's just for you? The actual act of cooking—with the right tools, ingredients, tips, and, most important, mindset—doesn't have to be difficult. In fact, it can be very enjoyable. Just like finishing an awesome workout, getting a haircut, or meditating in the morning, cooking for yourself is another form of self-care.

Cooking for yourself—as opposed to constantly ordering takeout—means you can control your ingredients, which means you can control your waistline and budget. Maybe that's in the form of adding more vegetables to a dish, reducing your salt intake by reaching for herbs and lemons instead, or building flavorful meals with just a few inexpensive pantry items. By consuming meals that are balanced in terms of color, variety, flavor, and texture—and portioned correctly—it's much easier to avoid overeating.

Cooking can help boost our mental health, too. When we step away from our screens, flip on some music, maybe pour a glass of wine, and carve out a little time to just be with ourselves in the kitchen, cooking can be an extremely meditative, pleasurable activity. After all, cooking ignites every single one of our senses: We see the brightly colored vegetables, smell the chopped fresh garlic and herbs, hear a sizzling steak, and, of course, enjoy the taste of it all.

I began cooking for myself in college while studying abroad in London. I had two cents (or I guess I should say two pence) to my name at the time, so daily restaurant takeout was not an option. My program didn't have an included meal plan, so I had to really think about how to prepare affordable, healthy meals for myself during the week. This allowed me to splurge on going out at other times while also avoiding the late-night-pizza-induced "sophomore fifteen."

Cooking for myself took on a different meaning as I got closer to and into my early thirties. I was very active, participating in triathlons and enjoying the dawn of high-intensity interval training. Preparing healthy meals was a way to nourish myself after a hard workout or work week. It also helped me continue to maximize my food budget and reduce waste so I could enjoy those occasional restaurant meals out—or ordered in.

When I met my husband, although I began technically cooking for two, the basics and fundamentals never changed. Now that we have two young kids, I still feel like I'm cooking for one or two sometimes (given how picky the kids are right now!), but with the benefit of understanding how to shop on a budget, get creative with leftovers, and maximize freezer space. There are some nights when my husband is out, and I'm fine with using up leftovers; other times, he might want a steak and I'd like a quinoa salad. Even if you don't live alone, maybe you want to escape your roommates; retreating to the kitchen is a great way to do that.

Easy, home-cooked, properly sized meals are within reach; all it takes is a little knowhow in the grocery store and kitchen, and for that, this book is here to help. All the recipes can be made within 30 minutes or less and many are one-pan dishes without the need for any specialty ingredients or fancy tools and techniques. Now, let's get cooking!

CHAPTER 1

Making Time for Yourself

Cooking for yourself is all about making time for yourself. It means you are putting yourself first, nourishing both your body and soul. Cooking for yourself, however, can only be one of life's greatest pleasures when it doesn't add to your already full plate outside the kitchen. In this chapter, you'll learn how to set yourself up for no-stress success.

EFFICIENT COOKING FOR ONE

Whether you're a novice cook or an experienced home chef, you might be new to solo cooking. This book provides quick, healthy, and delicious recipes to get you started, as well as advice on how to strategically meal plan and shop for one to make things as quick and easy as possible. The goal of this book is to give you the tools you need to cook for yourself at home without waste or leftovers—and feel confident doing so. Most important, you'll learn how to create meals that are simply yummy!

We'll go over a variety of tips and tricks, but the upcoming sections cover these five important lessons:

Planning ahead (page 3): Meal planning is especially helpful when cooking for one because it helps you map out the week and figure out how you'll use the same ingredient two or more times to reduce waste and stretch your budget.

Building your pantry (page 4): Once you have some key items on hand, you'll be able to pull together a meal in no time and with minimal effort.

Shopping smart (page 6): This section offers tips for how to shop without buying too much and for cooking with smaller portions.

Making the most of ingredients (page 8): From properly storing herbs to getting acquainted with your freezer, you'll find some ways to reduce waste.

Becoming a faster chef (page 11): After a little practice and visualization, you'll know how much a tablespoon is, how much salt or spice to use (to your preference), or how to just grab a handful of herbs or nuts, chop them, and garnish on the fly.

Fast but Not Furious

This book is designed to set you up with the right know-how and resources to be able to cook with ease and, most important, with joy. Even if you have never enjoyed cooking or don't feel like you have the patience to relish it right now, I promise you'll discover how enjoyable cooking for yourself can be, especially if you approach it with a positive mindset and establish a routine. It's kind of like going to the gym: It's hard to get there, but once you get into the groove and finish your workout, you feel great. The same rule applies here: Once you get into the kitchen, make it a pleasurable experience, like a date night with yourself.

Here are some ideas:

- Put on your favorite tunes, preferably with an upbeat sound to get you going.
- Crack open some wine (or your favorite beverage) for simultaneous cooking and sipping.
- Take photos to share with your friends and family or just to keep track of your progress.
- Set up your workspace right. Keep it tidy, cleaning as you go.
- Invite some inspiration. Decorate your kitchen with fun kitchen towels, pretty artwork, a big bowl of colorful fruit or bouquet of flowers . . . whatever inspires you.
- Don't forget that you don't have to cook everything this second. Cooking, like many activities, is a craft that takes repetition, consistency, and practice.

MEAL PLANNING

The first step in meal planning is, well, meal planning. But you don't have to make a spreadsheet! And, rest assured, most recipes here call for ingredients that can be used up in a single recipe. Still, having a basic roadmap for the week ahead will maximize your time, minimize waste, and prevent impulse buying. Here are some tips:

Pick meals that use similar ingredients. Planning on making Stuffed Peppers with Spiced Beans, Quinoa, and Cilantro Cream (page 62)? Consider making Pepper and Egg Muffin Cups (page 23) or Ratatouille Pasta with Torn Basil (page 69) that week, too, so you can use up your bell peppers. I like to zero in on vegetables shared by different recipes to use those up before they go bad. Extra meat can always be frozen.

Plan your leftovers. Most of these recipes are optimized to reduce leftovers. But if you do find yourself with some, instead of just spooning them out of the container cold, think about how you can be more creative. For example, leftover cooked fish can easily become the filling for Fish Tacos with Quick-Pickled Red Onions and Smoky Chili Cream (page 38). You'll find tips like this throughout the book.

Use produce wisely. Plan your meals around the produce that will go bad the fastest. Use delicate greens and spinach first, followed by cruciferous vegetables, peppers, and tender squashes like zucchini and yellow squash, followed by root vegetables. I also like to "empty out" my produce bin at the end of the week, using extra veggies for salads and bowls, soups, frittatas, and tacos.

Try a new dish each week. It's easy to get in a rut and make the same thing over and over. That's fine in general, but too much of it is boring. Try to pick one or two new dishes you might want to try each week; it's even better if they share some of the same ingredients.

Keep notes. I use a cloud-based notes app that I can access on my phone easily when I'm at home or at the store to keep a running grocery list as well as some meal ideas. But you can do whatever works for you to help you stay organized.

BUILDING YOUR PANTRY

A thoughtfully stocked pantry will help you cook a tasty, well-balanced meal with what you have on hand. You can also round out a meal when you have extra beans, leftover meat, and some veggies. To maintain your pantry, take inventory of what's running low before heading out to shop in case some items need to be restocked.

To make things as easy as possible for you to get started, I have limited this list. Slowly build your pantry as you try a few recipes.

OIL
- Avocado (healthiest for high-heat cooking)
- Coconut
- Olive, extra-virgin

VINEGAR
- Apple cider
- Balsamic

CANNED/JARRED/BOXED
- Beans: black, cannellini, chickpeas, kidney
- Broth: chicken, beef, vegetable
- Coconut milk, unsweetened
- Hot sauce

- Mustard: Dijon
- Soy sauce
- Tomatoes: diced, paste
- Tuna

BAKING
- Baking soda
- Baking powder
- Chocolate, dark
- Flour: all-purpose, whole-wheat
- Maple syrup, pure
- Vanilla extract, pure

DRIED
- Lentils, red
- Panko bread crumbs
- Pasta noodles
- Quinoa, rolled oats, farro
- Rice: long-grain white, brown

NUTS/SEEDS
- Almond/peanut butter
- Almonds, cashews, and walnuts, unsalted
- Tahini

DAIRY/EGGS
- Butter, unsalted
- Cheese: Cheddar, feta, mozzarella, Parmesan
- Eggs, large
- Milk/nondairy milk
- Yogurt, plain Greek

FRUITS/VEGETABLES

- Garlic
- Lemons
- Onions: red, yellow

HERBS/SPICES

- Cumin, ground
- Garlic powder
- Peppercorns, black
- Red pepper flakes
- Sea salt

An Ode to Canned Goods

Oh, how I love canned (and jarred) goods. These little gems of joy are great for convenience purposes, and although they might have gotten a bad rap in years past, there are now many organic, "clean," and preservative-free options with low or no salt added, many of which are also canned in BPA-free containers, so you can keep in line with your health goals. It's incredible how a can of fire-roasted tomatoes and green chiles can make your chili pop. Even just plain old canned tomatoes can taste amazing when simmered with garlic, onion, herbs, and balsamic drizzle. Canned beans, roasted red peppers, and artichoke hearts add nutrients to any dish. Knowing how to use a whole jar can be challenging, though. If you only need a portion of tomatoes, for example, the rest will be fine wrapped tightly with plastic wrap in the refrigerator for use later that week, or you can transfer them to a jar for a couple weeks. For longer-term storage, freeze leftovers in resealable plastic bags marked with the date of use.

SMART SHOPPING

Your best bet for healthy shopping is the store's perimeter, which generally includes the produce, fish, meat, dairy, and deli sections, although food makers now offer a few convenient items that are still "healthy," such as jarred minced garlic, fresh lemon juice, par-cooked whole grains, sugar-free marinara, etc. Before you head out, consider organizing your shopping list into categories (produce, meat/fish, dairy, grains/bulk) so you can shop the grocery store efficiently.

PRODUCE

With so many stores offering a wider variety of vegetables and organics, it's pretty easy to pluck a pepper or two, some mushrooms by the pound, and other produce in bulk. Purchase prewashed, packaged greens as well as prechopped veggies for quicker cooking. For smaller portions of prechopped veggies, head to the salad bar. I'm even seeing items like roasted beets and roasted artichokes—two veggies that take some time to cook. Many frozen fruits and veggies are a fine option also because they are flash-frozen at harvest. Load up on frozen berries for smoothies, and frozen peas and corn, but avoid high-moisture frozen veggies like bell peppers, mushrooms, and asparagus; they don't thaw as well.

MEAT, POULTRY, AND SEAFOOD

When shopping for one, visit the butcher and fishmonger counters. These experts not only can portion smaller pieces but also offer advice on how best to clean, store, prepare, and cook different cuts of meat and types of fish. If you end up purchasing some poultry or meat on sale, portion it into individual bags before freezing so you can pull one out as needed. Also, consider asking for a small bag of ice to keep your fish fresh while you continue shopping and head home. Some grocery seafood items have been previously frozen and thawed at the store, so don't re-freeze them.

BEANS, GRAINS, AND DRIED GOODS

Though it's great to stock up on canned cooked beans for convenience, the bulk aisle is the best place for purchasing dried beans, grains, rice, nuts, seeds, cereals, and more in smaller batches. It's often more cost-effective to buy dried goods this way rather than getting stuck with huge bags of rice. When you get home, transfer and store these items in resealable plastic bags or airtight containers for maximum freshness.

DAIRY

Look for small cartons of milk and cream. Many nut milks come in smaller packages, so you're covered there. At the cheese counter, don't feel like you have to go with the giant hunk of Parmesan; you can ask staff to cut smaller portions of most cheeses and rewrap them for you. Some stores even maintain piles of leftover cheeses after cutting that are usually smaller in size. Grab some crackers, and boom! Instant cheese board appetizer for one.

MAKING THE MOST OF INGREDIENTS

The recipes in this book have you covered in terms of using up ingredients, but knowing how to store ingredients properly will go a long way when cooking solo. Below are some guidelines for storing common ingredients so they don't go to waste.

Take advantage of the freezer. Freeze bread, chopped onions, anchovies, chipotle chiles, beans, butter, cheese—even nuts and seeds. Collect bones and veggie scraps for making chicken or veggie stock. Divide bulk purchases of chicken or meat into individual portions. Freeze cooked rice and grains in individual portions, and use ice cube trays to freeze leftover wine, stock, and herbs mixed with oil, for pan sauces.

Preserve your herbs. Rinse fresh herbs in cool water, trim an inch off the stems, and set them upright in a jar filled with water. Cover the leaves with a plastic bag and transfer them to the refrigerator. Or dry them in the microwave: Place between two paper towels, microwave on high for 2 minutes, crush, and transfer to an airtight container.

Turn quickly ripening fruit into dessert. Bananas or apples ripening faster than you wanted? Make Maple-Banana Bread Pudding (page 119) or Baked Cinnamon-Apple Crisp (page 118)! Or peel bananas, cut them in half, and freeze them in a plastic bag for smoothies. For avocados, make Cucumber-Avocado Toast with Balsamic and Black Pepper (page 18) or transfer them to the refrigerator where they'll last a few more days.

Arrange the refrigerator by expiration date. Follow the grocery store rule: first in, first out. Put jars and items with later expiration dates toward the back and keep the items with nearer expiration dates to the front so you're reminded to use those up sooner. If you have two of the same item, keep the one with the earlier expiration date closer to the front.

Use the proper storage materials. Plastic bags can speed up decay, so remove veggies when you get home. Wrap fresh greens in a damp paper towel and transfer to a resealable plastic bag. For leftovers, consider using microwave-safe glass containers rather than plastic because some studies have shown that microwaving plastic can cause chemicals to leach into food.

Wait to wash (or chop). Consider rinsing fruit and veggies only moments before you prep them because excess moisture can speed decay. Also, don't prep more than you need at a time. For example, if you have a head of lettuce, tear or cut the leaves off, leaving the bulb intact. The same goes for onions: If dicing only half of them, don't peel or chop the half you don't plan to use immediately.

Restrain from tossing. Don't throw out that Parmesan cheese rind! Add it to your pasta water for extra umami flavor. Save the pickle jar and add slices of cucumber to the pickling liquid so they'll last longer. Or, chop up cucumbers and tomatoes that are ripening too quickly and marinate them in extra-virgin olive oil and balsamic for extra preservation (see Marinated Vegetable Salad with Fresh Mozzarella, page 31).

TOOLS AND EQUIPMENT

Cooking solo is much easier when you have a few kitchen equipment essentials on hand. Avoid nonstick skillets, which scratch easily and can expose toxic chemicals. I prefer aluminum or ceramic for everyday sautéing and definitely cast iron for meats and high-heat searing. Although not necessary for the recipes in this book, consider investing in a toaster oven. They preheat faster and can cook foods more quickly than traditional ovens.

This book assumes you already have these basic kitchen necessities:

- Chopping board
- Kitchen shears
- Knives + sharpening tool
- Medium colander
- Oven mitts
- Rubber and metal spatulas
- Rubber-coated tongs
- Slotted spoon
- Wire whisk
- Wooden spoon

Here are some other things you might want to consider purchasing; if you already have larger versions of these items, that'll still work, although smaller cooking vessels cook food faster.

3- or 4-quart saucepan and lid: For soups, small batches of pasta, and steaming or blanching veggies.

3.5-inch (or larger) deep skillet and lid: This pan is great for great for sautéing and simmering or cooking with liquid. Nonstick is okay, or consider ceramic or a good quality Dutch oven.

5-by-9-inch loaf pan: For mini casseroles and smaller baked desserts.

6.5-inch cast-iron skillet and/or griddle: I love cast iron for meat cooking; you can create a nicely seared crust and then transfer the skillet to a high-heat oven or broiler. I recommend one with deep sides so you can also make great pan sauces in the same pot.

6-unit muffin pan: Perfect for small batches of muffins.

8-by-8-inch glass baking dish: Perfect for smaller portions of fish and vegetables as well as casseroles.

8-inch oven-safe skillet: Great for smaller-batch cooking, like eggs and omelets for one, small pan sauces, or sautéing veggies quicker.

10-inch oven-safe sauté pan/skillet and lid: This will be your go-to most nights.

Blender and food processor/mini food processor: If I had to choose, I'd pick a food processor; they really cut down on time and effort, and you can still make smoothies and soups in them.

Digital thermometer: It's always a good idea to let a thermometer tell you when meat is at the proper temp.

Graters: Box grater for shredding cheese. Microplane for zesting citrus and quick-grating Parmesan over a dish.

Measuring cups and utensils: For smaller portions, you'll want a set of measuring spoons that includes ⅛ teaspoon, ½ teaspoon, and ½ tablespoon. Also, I prefer microwave-safe liquid glass containers (1 cup and a 2- or 3-cup).

Ramekins: 3.5- and 6.5-ounce ramekins are great for single-serve desserts and make useful small containers when prepping ingredients.

Rimmed baking sheets: Available in 9-by-13-inch and smaller.

Specialty utensils: A good fish spatula, handheld juicer, meat mallet, and a microwave-safe, vented cover are handy. You might also invest in a handheld immersion blender.

GETTING FASTER IN THE KITCHEN

The more I cook, the faster at it I get. Let me share a few tips that have helped make me a more efficient cook. These techniques will help you maximize your time and effort while keeping your workspace organized and tidy.

Read through the recipe before you commit to it. How many times have you started working on a recipe only to discover halfway through cooking that you don't have that extra casserole dish or you need to marinate the meat overnight?

Prepare all ingredients before you start cooking. This is called *mise en place*, meaning "everything in its place." Chop and place veggies in separate small bowls (putting them on a small tray is a good idea). You might not have to measure out 1 tablespoon of soy sauce or teaspoon of spice ahead of time (to save yourself from washing endless ramekins), but keep the bottles and a measuring spoon near the stove so everything's at hand.

Learn how to eyeball measurements. Try measuring portions of dried ingredients into your palm a few times to visualize how much a teaspoon or tablespoon is. Baking requires very precise measurements, so don't wing it there.

ABM (Always Be Multitasking). While preheating the oven, prep your ingredients. While something is roasting, clean up the kitchen. Bake a potato for tomorrow's lunch while making pasta for dinner. I wrap a head of garlic (top sliced off and drizzled with a little extra-virgin olive oil) in aluminum foil and roast it alongside whatever's in the oven so I can use it later as a flavor booster for sauces, dressings, or as a schmear for bread and veggies.

Make easy substitutions. Even if a recipe calls for a certain type of ingredient, you can probably use what you have on hand. Use avocado, canola, grapeseed, and vegetable oils for searing meats, and extra-virgin olive oil and nut oils for lower-temp cooking, dressings, and garnishes. Most nuts and cheeses can be swapped, but for recipes that call for melting cheese, it's best to choose a substitute of the same cheese type.

TIME-SAVING PREP

There are some prepping methods that you'll use again and again. These tips and tricks will save you a lot of time.

Handling knives: You can hold a knife by the handle, but a "blade grip" is how they taught us in culinary school, and it's better for more precision cuts (and more protection, once you get it right). Grip the top portion of the blade closest to the handle with your thumb and a bent index finger, almost like chopsticks, allowing your other fingers to gently wrap around the handle of the blade. Put pressure on your thumb and index finger to hold the knife while allowing the other fingers to just guide the blade. When slicing and chopping food, always protect your fingertips by curling them inward, which allows your knuckles to guide the knife.

Dicing onions: Halve the onion vertically. Peel the outer layers and discard them. Working with one half at a time, with the cut side facing you, make incisions running from the bulb to the cut side, left to right, about ¼-inch apart. Carefully make incisions going from the cut side toward the bulb through the onion's middle. Then, slice from the cut side toward the bulb crosswise. Diced pieces will magically appear.

Mincing garlic: Smash the clove with the flat side of your knife blade, then peel it. Slice the clove super thin (keeping your nails tucked under and your knuckles forward). Then, with the tip of your knife touching the cutting board, rest your free hand on top of the blade while rocking it up and down to finely chop, scraping the pieces along the chopping board occasionally to form a paste.

Chiffonade: Stack herb or baby spinach leaves on top of each other, roll them up like a cigar, and thinly slice them crosswise.

Deglazing: After searing a protein, remove it, add an acid (vinegar, wine, or stock) to the pan, and scrape up the browned bits from the bottom with a wooden spoon.

Zesting and juicing: Grate the zest from lemons and limes right over a bowl with a microplane, avoiding the bitter white pith. Then halve the fruit and squeeze the juice.

THE RECIPES IN THIS BOOK

These recipes are designed to be satisfying, healthy meals for one average adult, with minimal leftovers. But there are a few specific types of recipe that will help you speed up your meal prep or give you more flexibility.

RECIPE TIPS

Throughout the recipe chapters, you'll find tips for what to do when a recipe doesn't use all of an ingredient, preparation tips, information tips about an ingredient, and suggestions on how to make the dish even more quickly.

RECIPE LABELS

In a Pinch: A few recipes per chapter will be labeled "In a Pinch." These recipes take 20 minutes or less to prep and make.

Good for Scaling: Want leftovers or expecting company? Some recipes are particularly well-suited for scaling to two servings to use up an entire ingredient, cook for a guest, or give you lunch the next day. For these recipes, all you need to do is double the quantities and note that the cooking time will increase by about double as well.

A Few Recipes to Try Now

These are some of my favorite recipes that fill my different moods and cravings.

If you want a takeout-inspired meal for movie night, try Pork Noodles with Chili Oil (page 98) or Tofu and Snow Pea Stir-Fry with Soba Noodles (page 63).

If you're craving pizza but want a healthier option, try Flatbread with Prosciutto, Goat Cheese, and Broccoli (page 42).

If you feel like breakfast for dinner, go for Ham, Egg, and Cheese Skillet Sandwich (page 24), or Salsa-Baked Eggs (page 22), or Two-Egg Omelet with Goat Cheese and Chives (page 21) with crusty bread and a side salad.

If you had a bad day and want something warm, comforting, and still guilt-free, try Chicken and Rice Noodle Soup (page 55), Very Tomatoey Soup with Parmesan Crisp (page 49), or Tangy Onion Soup, and don't forget the cheese toast (page 56)!

Easy Breakfasts

< Berry Smoothie Bowl with Toppers,
  page 17

EASY GREEN SMOOTHIE

IN A PINCH / PREP TIME: 5 MINUTES, PLUS UP TO 90 SECONDS TO BLEND

This is my go-to "break the fast" meal when I need to power up for the day with a dose of nutrients. The avocado adds vitamin E for skin health and a little healthy fat to keep you satisfied. Adding spinach doesn't change the flavor, and it's loaded with vitamin C and calcium.

¼ medium avocado

1 small banana, frozen

2 cups packed baby spinach

1 cup milk (or unsweetened nut milk)

½ cup ice

Combine all the ingredients in a blender. Blend until smooth, 60 to 90 seconds. Pour into a glass and enjoy. Add cold, filtered water to thin, as needed.

Use It Up: Enjoy the rest of the avocado as a topper for soup or salad for lunch or make Cucumber-Avocado Toast with Balsamic and Black Pepper (page 18) the next day. Otherwise, to preserve freshness, run a knife around the middle of the avocado to halve it. Scoop the flesh from a quarter of it into the blender. Put the halves back together with the pit intact, tightly wrap, and refrigerate for later use.

BERRY SMOOTHIE BOWL WITH TOPPERS

IN A PINCH / PREP TIME: 5 MINUTES, PLUS UP TO 90 SECONDS TO BLEND

This is another go-to breakfast when I want something a little more filling than a smoothie but that's still fresh and light. I can almost feel my skin brightening after I eat this, especially if I top the antioxidant-rich bowl with kiwi slices, which have as much or more vitamin C than oranges. This bowl is also great for a post-workout meal; the banana delivers a dose of potassium and the nut butter keeps you full longer.

1 cup frozen berries (blueberries, raspberries, or a combination)

1 small banana, frozen and peeled

2 tablespoons almond (or peanut) butter

¾ cup canned, full-fat coconut milk

½ cup plain Greek yogurt

Pinch ground cinnamon

Toppings (optional): chopped nuts, granola, sliced fresh fruit, unsweetened coconut flakes

1. Combine the berries, banana, almond butter, coconut milk, yogurt, and cinnamon in a blender and pulse until smooth, 60 to 90 seconds.
2. Pour into a bowl, top with your favorite toppings, and enjoy.

CUCUMBER-AVOCADO TOAST WITH BALSAMIC AND BLACK PEPPER

IN A PINCH / PREP TIME: 5 MINUTES / COOK TIME: 5 MINUTES

Avocado toast, like smoothies, has endless options for variations. You could top it with toasted sesame oil, sesame seeds, and scallions; pomegranate seeds for a tangy, juicy punch; smoked salmon and "everything but the bagel" seasoning; or hot sauce and cilantro, just to name a few. Add a fried (or microwaved) egg or even a little crumbled bacon for extra protein.

1 thick slice bread (sturdy whole grain or sourdough)

½ medium avocado

½ teaspoon balsamic vinegar

4 thin cucumber slices

½ teaspoon extra-virgin olive oil (optional)

¼ teaspoon freshly ground black pepper, plus a pinch for topping

1. Toast the bread until it's golden.
2. Halve the avocado lengthwise and remove the pit. Use a large spoon to scoop the avocado flesh into a small bowl, add the vinegar, and mash it with the back of a fork.
3. Layer the cucumber slices on the bread. Spread mashed avocado on top.
4. Top with the olive oil (if using) and pepper. Enjoy.

Use It Up: Chop up leftover cucumber for Marinated Vegetable Salad with Fresh Mozzarella (page 31) or Lemony Hummus Bowl with Cucumber-Tomato-Feta Salad (page 66).

OVERNIGHT OATS AND CHIA

PREP TIME: 5 MINUTES, PLUS 12 HOURS TO REFRIGERATE

This jar of goodies is such a nice surprise to wake up to when I've remembered to mix it up the night before, or even a few days prior. You can add anything from fresh berries and banana, nuts, peanut butter, a little yogurt, and even unsweetened coconut flakes, but I recommend adding them just before you eat the oats so they won't get soggy. Overnight oats will keep in the refrigerator (without toppings) for up to 5 days.

¼ cup old-fashioned rolled oats

½ tablespoon chia seeds

Pinch ground cinnamon

¾ cup milk or nondairy milk

1 teaspoon maple syrup or honey (optional)

1. In a clean mason or other glass jar with a lid (large enough to have room for the oats and chia to expand), add the oats, chia seeds, and cinnamon. Pour in the milk. Stir well to combine or screw the lid on top and shake. Refrigerate overnight.

2. The next day, add maple syrup (if using) or another sweetener (if desired) and stir the oats well. Add any additional toppings of choice and enjoy.

Tip: I added chia seeds to this recipe because they absorb liquid well, making the consistency more pudding-like, plus they offer a dose of healthy omega-3 fatty acids. If you ever just want chia and no oats, follow the 3-tablespoons-to-1-cup-milk ratio. For a warm breakfast, simply microwave the jar (if it's microwave-safe) covered with a paper towel for 1 to 2 minutes.

SCRAMBLED MUG EGGS WITH CHICKEN SAUSAGE AND SPINACH

IN A PINCH / PREP TIME: 5 MINUTES, PLUS 90 SECONDS TO MICROWAVE

When I'm really hungry and short on time, this is a super easy protein-packed breakfast or even light lunch option. Just watch the eggs closely and stir frequently because some microwaves are hotter than others. You might also want to cook at a lower power just to prevent a blow-up!

2 large eggs

1 precooked chicken sausage link, thinly sliced

¼ cup thinly sliced spinach leaves

Shredded cheese (optional)

Hot sauce (optional)

Chopped fresh cilantro (optional)

Diced avocado (optional)

1. Crack the eggs into a large mug. Beat them well with a fork. Stir in the chicken sausage and spinach.

2. Cover the mug and microwave on high, breaking up the eggs with the fork every 20 seconds, until just cooked through, about 90 seconds.

3. Top with cheese, hot sauce, cilantro, and avocado, if using, and enjoy.

TWO-EGG OMELET WITH GOAT CHEESE AND CHIVES

IN A PINCH / PREP TIME: 5 MINUTES / COOK TIME: 5 MINUTES

I learned the technique for making this classic French omelet in culinary school. My French chef-instructor at the time said he would enjoy this omelet often, usually for brunch or even light lunch when paired with a small salad—a tuft of frisée lettuce tossed lightly with a touch of extra-virgin olive oil, splash of lemon juice or red wine vinegar, and a sprinkling of coarse salt and freshly ground black pepper. Crusty bread or toast optional.

4 tablespoons unsalted butter

2 large eggs

Pinch salt

2 tablespoons goat cheese, at room temperature

Freshly ground black pepper

Chopped fresh chives (or any other herbs you have on hand), for garnish

1. Melt the butter in the microwave on low. With a metal spoon, skim the frothy white whey off the top and discard, setting aside the clear, clarified butter.

2. In a small bowl, beat the eggs with a fork until frothy. Beat in the salt.

3. Heat the clarified butter in a small skillet over medium-low heat. Pour in the eggs. With the same fork used to beat the eggs, gently stir the eggs until they begin to set on the bottom. Pause to let the eggs set completely, 3 minutes.

4. Spoon the goat cheese into the center of the omelet. Using the same fork, immediately flip the left side over onto the middle of the omelet; repeat with the right side. The eggs should be a touch runny in the middle.

5. Carefully flip the pan over a plate so the omelet lands, filling-side down, on the plate.

6. Sprinkle with the pepper, garnish with the herbs, and enjoy.

SALSA-BAKED EGGS

IN A PINCH / PREP TIME: 5 MINUTES / COOK TIME: 15 MINUTES

This is an easy, set-it-and-forget-it breakfast (or lunch or dinner!) option that uses salsa to poach eggs for a flavorful, low-fat option. Top it off with a little fresh cilantro and avocado to round out the meal, and serve with crusty bread or tortillas, if desired. You could even sprinkle a little cheese over the top and let it melt during the last minute of baking.

½ cup prepared salsa (red or green)

2 large eggs

1 scallion, thinly sliced (green parts only)

Salt

Freshly ground black pepper

Avocado slices and/or chopped fresh cilantro, for garnish (optional)

1. Preheat the oven to 400°F.
2. Pour the salsa into a small loaf pan or small glass baking dish.
3. Carefully break the eggs, one by one, into the salsa so they sit side-by-side. Sprinkle the scallion over the eggs and season with the salt and pepper to taste.
4. Bake until the egg whites are cooked and the yolks are still runny, 15 minutes.
5. Serve immediately, topped with avocado and cilantro (if using).

PEPPER AND EGG MUFFIN CUPS

PREP TIME: 5 MINUTES / COOK TIME: 20 MINUTES, PLUS 5 MINUTES TO COOL / MAKES 6 MUFFINS

These protein- and veggie-packed "muffins" are great for breakfasts on the go, and this recipe will leave you with extras that can be refrigerated or frozen for later use. I usually make these on weekends to enjoy during a busy week. You can also top them with avocado, cilantro, salsa, and/or hot sauce to make them more of a meal and satisfy you for longer—or add ham or bacon for more protein.

12 large eggs

2 teaspoons salt

2 teaspoons freshly ground black pepper

1 medium red bell pepper, diced into ¼-inch-thick pieces

1 medium orange, yellow, or green bell pepper, diced into ¼-inch-thick pieces

½ cup thinly sliced scallions (green parts only)

1 small jalapeño, stemmed, seeded, and finely chopped (optional)

½ cup shredded cheddar cheese (optional)

1. Preheat the oven to 350°F. Thoroughly grease a 6-well muffin pan, or line with paper muffin liners.

2. In a large bowl, beat the eggs until they are fluffy. Whisk in the salt and pepper. Fold in the bell peppers, scallions, and jalapeño (if using), stirring to combine.

3. Ladle the egg mixture evenly into the prepared muffin pan. Top evenly with the cheese (if using).

4. Bake until a toothpick or paring knife inserted in the center comes out clean, 20 minutes. Let the muffins cool in the pan for 5 minutes.

5. Cut around the edges of each muffin to loosen, and lift them out using a small rubber spatula or flat-edged knife. Enjoy warm or cool completely and transfer to a container or resealable plastic bag for storing in the freezer.

Tip: Did you know you can regrow scallions on your windowsill? After cutting off the green parts of the stalks, leave the roots intact and place them upright in a jar or glass filled with water. Set it by a natural light source and refresh the water every couple of days. Cut off the green parts as they regrow, leaving the white part and roots intact. With enough light and water, they should regrow a few times.

HAM, EGG, AND CHEESE SKILLET SANDWICH

IN A PINCH / PREP TIME: 5 MINUTES / COOK TIME: 10 MINUTES

This is a super fun French-toast-meets-omelet-meets-gooey-ham-and-cheese sandwich that's both savory and a little sweet. It's also very portable. It requires a little finesse to flip the eggs and bread together, but it's a cool trick when you can pull it off. I call for sharp cheddar for a pop of flavor, but you could use any other cheese you have on hand or a combination of cheeses.

3 large eggs

⅛ teaspoon salt

⅛ teaspoon freshly ground black pepper

⅛ teaspoon ground nutmeg

2 tablespoons unsalted butter

2 slices bread of choice

2 slices sharp cheddar cheese

1 slice ham

2 teaspoons thinly sliced chives

1. In a medium bowl, whisk the eggs until frothy. Add the salt, pepper, and nutmeg and whisk to combine.

2. Melt the butter in a 10- or 12-inch skillet over medium-low heat. Pour in the eggs. Coat both sides of the bread in the egg mixture and place the slices next to each other in the skillet. Cook, running a spatula around the edges, until the eggs are just set on the bottom, 5 minutes.

3. When set, slide a flat spatula underneath the eggs, guiding with another spatula on top, and carefully flip over the eggs and bread as one.

4. Fold the top and bottom egg layers over the bread slices and then the sides to envelop the slices in the cooked egg. Layer 1 slice of cheese and then the ham on the right-hand piece of bread. Top with the remaining cheese slice and chives. Cover and cook until the cheese begins to melt and the eggs set, 1 minute.

5. Fold the left slice over the right to close the sandwich. Cover and continue to cook until the cheese has melted, 1 minute more.

6. Transfer the sandwich to a chopping board, slice in half, and enjoy.

Tip: Chop up any leftover ham and add it to Pepper and Egg Muffin Cups (page 23), or you can always skip the ham or substitute thinly sliced bacon. Add spinach if you're looking for an extra pop of green.

CHEESY BLACK BEAN BREAKFAST BURRITO

IN A PINCH / PREP TIME: 5 MINUTES / COOK TIME: 10 MINUTES

Have leftover beans? Try out this easy handheld breakfast. Everything gets rolled up together in the tortilla that's then toasted shut for convenient, flavor-packed enjoyment.

1 tablespoon unsalted butter

2 large eggs, beaten

½ cup canned black beans, drained and rinsed

¼ cup shredded cheddar cheese, or more if needed

1 (7- or 8-inch) flour tortilla

2 tablespoons prepared salsa of choice (or 3 dashes hot sauce)

2 tablespoons chopped fresh cilantro

1. Melt the butter in an 8-inch skillet over medium-low heat. Add the eggs and beans, gently stirring constantly with a rubber spatula until the eggs are lightly scrambled and just about to set, 5 minutes.

2. Sprinkle the cheese over the eggs, cover the skillet, and continue cooking until the cheese is starting to melt, 1 minute.

3. Place the tortilla on a work surface or plate. Spoon the egg mixture onto the center of the tortilla. Top with the salsa and cilantro.

4. Fold in the sides of the tortilla over the filling, using your thumbs to bring up the bottom of the tortilla, then roll up the tortilla tightly.

5. Place the burrito, seam-side down, in the skillet and toast over medium heat until brown and tightly sealed, 2 minutes. Flip and continue toasting until brown on the other side. Enjoy immediately.

Tip: If you only have smaller tortillas, divide the egg mixture between two 4-inch tortillas and enjoy them like tacos. Burritos and tacos can also be made ahead, wrapped, and stored in the refrigerator for a few days. Microwave on high for 60 to 90 seconds to reheat.

SAVORY CREPE WITH SCALLIONS, SESAME, AND CHILE-SPIKED CREAM CHEESE

GOOD FOR SCALING / PREP TIME: 10 MINUTES / COOK TIME: 20 MINUTES

This recipe is loosely inspired by Chinese bing pancakes, a popular street food made from a doughy batter that's flattened thin, cooked on a hot griddle, and often rolled up with an egg, fermented bean paste, and/or chili-garlic sauce, scallions, and cilantro. Here, an eggier, crepe-like batter offers a quicker substitute, with a similarly flattened shape and savory flavors. Double the recipe to make two crepes for a larger portion (or a friend).

2 tablespoons cream cheese, at room temperature

2 dashes hot sauce

⅛ teaspoon red pepper flakes

2 tablespoons all-purpose or gluten-free flour

1½ tablespoons milk or nondairy milk

1 large egg

Pinch salt

2 tablespoons unsalted butter

2 teaspoons sesame seeds

1 tablespoon chopped scallion (green part only)

1. In a small bowl, mix the cream cheese, hot sauce, and red pepper flakes with a fork. Set aside.

2. In a medium bowl, whisk together the flour, milk, egg, and salt until frothy.

3. Melt the butter in a skillet over medium-low heat. Pour in the batter. Cook until set on the bottom, the edges are beginning to curl, and the crepe easily moves around the pan, 2 to 3 minutes. Carefully flip and cook until set on the other side, 1 to 2 minutes more. Transfer the crepe to a serving plate.

4. Spread a dollop of the cream cheese mixture in a line down one side of the crepe, leaving ½ inch around the edges. Sprinkle the sesame seeds and scallion over the cream cheese.

5. Using a spatula, carefully roll the crepe from one side to the other. Enjoy warm.

PANCAKE "TACOS" WITH BACON, CHIVES, AND CHEESE

PREP TIME: 10 MINUTES / COOK TIME: 20 MINUTES / MAKES 2

I don't have a huge sweet tooth, but every now and then, I have a hankering for pancakes and crispy bacon. Good news: This recipe combines both of those comfort food faves, all wrapped up in handheld form (with a couple other goodies). Like many recipes in this book, variations abound: Substitute sausage for the bacon or go meat-free and add scrambled eggs. Or, enjoy the pancakes all on their own!

2 bacon slices (preferably nitrate-free)

⅓ cup all-purpose flour (or gluten-free flour)

1¼ teaspoons baking powder

Pinch salt

¼ cup milk

1 large egg

1 tablespoon unsalted butter, melted, cooled

½ teaspoon pure vanilla extract

2 teaspoons maple syrup, plus more for serving (optional)

2 tablespoons shredded cheddar cheese

2 teaspoons chopped fresh chives

1. Heat an 8-inch skillet over medium heat. Cook the bacon until crispy and the fat is rendered, flipping once, 6 minutes.

2. While the bacon cooks, in a medium bowl, whisk together the flour, baking powder, and salt. Set aside.

3. In a small bowl, whisk together the milk, egg, butter, vanilla, and maple syrup. Pour the wet ingredients into the dry and use a large spoon to stir until just combined.

4. Reduce the heat to medium-low and transfer the bacon to a paper towel–lined plate. Pour off all but 1 tablespoon of bacon fat into a small bowl or jar. Set aside.

5. Spoon half of the batter into the center of the skillet. Cook until bubbles form on the top of the pancake and the bottom is golden, 3 minutes. Flip and continue to cook until cooked through, 2 to 3 more minutes. Transfer the pancake to a serving plate. Top with 1 tablespoon of cheese, 1 teaspoon of chives, and 1 piece of bacon, broken in half. Close up like a taco.

6. Pour 1 tablespoon of the reserved fat into the skillet and repeat step 5 with the remaining pancake batter, cheese, bacon, and chives. Enjoy warm, with extra maple syrup (if using), or wrap each pancake in aluminum foil and take to go.

CHAPTER 3

Salads and Handhelds

< Crunchy Chickpea and Tahini Caesar Salad, page 33

CRUNCHY ENDIVE, CARROT, AND ORANGE SALAD WITH CREAMY CITRUS VINAIGRETTE

IN A PINCH / PREP TIME: 10 MINUTES

This bright and fresh salad always energizes my day, and it's a great way to sneak in a little extra vitamin C if you're feeling run-down. The recipe uses all parts of the orange, so none of it goes to waste, and its sweetness helps cut the bitterness of the endive.

1 small head endive, thinly sliced

1 medium carrot, peeled

1 large navel orange

2 teaspoons Dijon mustard

2 tablespoons extra-virgin olive oil

Salt

Freshly ground black pepper

2 tablespoons chopped fresh herbs (e.g., cilantro, basil, parsley, or a combination)

1. Put the endive in a serving bowl. Using a vegetable peeler, grate the carrot over the bowl to create shavings. Zest 1 teaspoon of orange peel into the bowl.

2. Remove and discard the rest of the peel by setting the orange upright on your chopping board and slicing around the orange, from top to bottom, turning it as you go, to reveal the flesh. Slice the orange in half lengthwise, and then, holding one half over the bowl with the salad ingredients, carefully pull apart the segments, dropping them into the bowl. It's okay if juice falls into the bowl; it will help flavor the salad.

3. Squeeze the juice from the other orange half into a separate small bowl or jar, and discard the flesh. Add the mustard, olive oil, salt, and pepper and whisk vigorously, or close the jar, if using, and shake to combine.

4. Pour the dressing over the salad, tossing to combine. Garnish with the herbs and enjoy.

Use It Up: Use leftover endive for Fish Tacos with Quick-Pickled Red Onions and Smoky Chili Cream (page 38) and any leftover grated carrot for Sticky Rice Bowl with Pickled Carrots, Cucumbers, and Fried Egg (page 70). Instead of discarding orange peel, use as a twist garnish for beverages and cocktails, add it to tea, or make a citrus-infused olive oil.

MARINATED VEGETABLE SALAD WITH FRESH MOZZARELLA

GOOD FOR SCALING / PREP TIME: 5 MINUTES, PLUS 20 MINUTES TO MARINATE

This is my go-to salad for when tomatoes and cucumbers are on their last days . . . or even hours. Artichoke hearts, olives, and fresh mozzarella round out the salad for a complete meal that can marinate overnight or longer, and feel free to double the recipe to have more to enjoy during the week. Add basil or other delicate herbs just before enjoying so they don't get soggy.

FOR THE DRESSING

¼ cup plus 1 tablespoon extra-virgin olive oil

1½ tablespoons balsamic vinegar

½ teaspoon Dijon mustard

¼ teaspoon freshly ground black pepper

½ teaspoon salt

FOR THE SALAD

1 teaspoon dried oregano

1 teaspoon dried thyme

½ pint cherry tomatoes, halved

1 small cucumber, diced

½ jar artichoke hearts, drained, coarsely chopped

3 tablespoons sliced, pitted black (or green) olives

½ mozzarella ball, cut into ¼-inch-thick pieces

Fresh basil and/or parsley, for garnish

TO MAKE THE DRESSING

1. In a large bowl, combine the olive oil, balsamic vinegar, Dijon mustard, black pepper, and salt. Whisk well to combine.

TO MAKE THE SALAD

2. Add the oregano, thyme, tomatoes, cucumber, artichoke hearts, olives, and mozzarella to the salad bowl, tossing to combine. Cover and refrigerate at least 20 minutes and up to 2 days.

3. To serve, toss the salad a few times to redistribute the dressing. Serve on a bed of lettuce, if desired. Garnish with herbs and extra black pepper and enjoy.

Ingredient Tip: Double the dressing ratio to have a delicious, "clean" balsamic dressing on hand for other salads and vegetable dishes (⅓ cup oil: 2 tablespoons balsamic vinegar: 1 teaspoon Dijon). Store in a jar with a lid and shake just before use.

Use It Up: The rest of the artichokes can be used for Spinach-Artichoke Loaded Potato (page 73).

SUPER GREEN SALAD WITH AVOCADO AND RASPBERRY VINAIGRETTE

IN A PINCH / PREP TIME: 10 MINUTES

A good friend of mine let me in on this dressing hack, which is perfect for adding more fruit to your daily intake. Tangy, naturally sweet raspberries also balance out the "greenness" of the greens and pair nicely with creamy avocado. As always, top this salad with whatever else you might have: chopped fresh herbs, cooked chicken or tofu, nuts or seeds, and goat cheese or feta.

½ cup fresh or frozen and thawed raspberries

1 tablespoon extra-virgin olive oil

1 tablespoon red wine vinegar

Salt

Freshly ground black pepper

2 to 3 cups loosely packed mixed baby greens (kale, spinach, arugula, etc.)

1 small avocado, pitted, peeled, and sliced

1. To make the dressing, combine the raspberries, olive oil, vinegar, salt, and pepper in a blender or food processor. Process until smooth, adding water by the teaspoonful to thin, if needed.

2. Place the greens in a serving bowl. Toss with the dressing. Top with avocado slices, additional optional ingredients, and more freshly ground black pepper. Enjoy.

Ingredient Tip: To quickly thaw frozen berries, microwave in a small microwave-safe bowl for 30 to 60 seconds on 50 percent power to prevent scorching.

CRUNCHY CHICKPEA AND TAHINI CAESAR SALAD

IN A PINCH / PREP TIME: 10 MINUTES / COOK TIME: 10 MINUTES

½ cup canned chickpeas, drained, rinsed, and patted dry

2 teaspoons extra-virgin olive oil

⅛ teaspoon salt, plus more for seasoning dressing

⅓ cup tahini paste

Juice of 1 lemon, plus more if desired

1 garlic clove, minced

Freshly ground black pepper

1 romaine heart, torn, or 2 to 3 cups torn romaine lettuce leaves

Parmesan cheese shavings, for garnish

1. Preheat the oven or toaster oven to 450°F.
2. Place the chickpeas on a small rimmed baking sheet. Toss with the olive oil and salt and spread out in a single layer. Roast them until they are brown and crispy, stirring once, for 10 minutes.
3. Meanwhile, in a small bowl, whisk together the tahini, lemon juice, and garlic. Add warm water, 1 tablespoon at a time, until the dressing is creamy. Season with the salt, pepper, and more lemon juice, if desired.
4. Remove the chickpeas from the oven and set aside. When ready to serve, place the lettuce in a large bowl. Toss with 2 to 3 tablespoons of dressing. Top with the chickpeas, more pepper, and Parmesan shavings. Enjoy.

Ingredient Tip: If working with a larger head of romaine, tear off the leaves but leave the bulb intact, rewrap in clean paper towels, and store in a resealable plastic bag in the crisper to last another day.

Use It Up: Drizzle leftover salad dressing over Lemony Hummus Bowl with Cucumber-Tomato-Feta Salad (page 66).

ROASTED BEET AND KALE SALAD WITH GOAT CHEESE, PISTACHIOS, AND TANGY DRESSING

PREP TIME: 10 MINUTES / COOK TIME: 15 MINUTES

Roasting beets normally takes forever, but slicing them thin before they go in the oven (and washing your hands and chopping board immediately afterward to prevent staining) helps reduce the time. All of this is worth it—beets are so good for you. They are loaded with antioxidants, fiber, potassium, iron, folate, and even "betalains," which are touted by athletes as aiding faster muscle recovery.

1 small to medium red beet bulb

2 tablespoons extra-virgin olive oil, divided

2 teaspoons red wine vinegar

1 teaspoon Dijon mustard

¼ teaspoon freshly ground black pepper, plus more for garnish

⅛ teaspoon salt

2 cups torn curly kale leaves

2 tablespoons roasted pistachios

1 ounce crumbled goat cheese (or feta)

1. Preheat the oven or toaster oven to 425°F.
2. Peel and slice the beet into ¼-inch-thick rounds. Place the slices on an aluminum foil–lined baking sheet, spaced about an inch apart. Roast until tender, 15 minutes.
3. Meanwhile, in a small bowl, whisk together 1 tablespoon of olive oil with the vinegar, mustard, pepper, and salt until creamy and set aside (or shake vigorously in a jar with a lid).
4. Place the kale in a large bowl. Drizzle the remaining 1 tablespoon of olive oil over the kale, and with clean hands, massage the leaves until coated and tender, 1 minute.
5. Remove the beet slices from the oven and place them on top of the kale leaves. Drizzle the dressing over the salad. Top with the pistachios and goat cheese and enjoy immediately.

Preparation Tip: Massaging the kale with the oil helps tenderize the leaves, making them easier to chew and digest. It also helps reduce any bitterness.

Use It Up: Leftover cheese can be used for Lemony Hummus Bowl with Cucumber-Tomato-Feta Salad (page 66) or Flatbread with Prosciutto, Goat Cheese, and Broccoli (page 42).

SPICY SHRIMP AND CORN ROLL

IN A PINCH / PREP TIME: 10 MINUTES / COOK TIME: 10 MINUTES

After a trip to Maine, I still dream about the buttery lobster rolls there. Lobster rolls are a huge point of controversy in the Northeast—some swear by only serving them warm, with drawn butter and that's it. Others prefer the meat to be chilled and lightly mixed with mayo and celery. We're meeting somewhere in the middle here, and we're swapping lobster for shrimp, which is less expensive and easier to come by year round. Corn adds some extra crunch and sweetness.

2 tablespoons unsalted butter

2 ounces small to medium raw shrimp, peeled and deveined

1 tablespoon thinly sliced celery

¼ cup frozen, thawed, or canned sweet corn, drained

⅛ teaspoon cayenne pepper

Pinch salt

Freshly ground black pepper

Juice of ½ lemon

2 teaspoons chopped fresh parsley, plus more for garnish

1 split-top hot dog or brioche sausage bun

Hot sauce (optional)

1. Melt the butter in a medium skillet over medium-low heat. Add the shrimp and cook until the butter begins to bubble and brown and the shrimp is pink on the outside and slightly firm to the touch, 5 minutes.

2. Stir in the celery, corn, and cayenne, season with salt and pepper, and pour the mixture into a small bowl, leaving a little butter in the skillet. Give the mixture another quick stir. When cooled slightly, fold in the lemon juice and parsley and set aside.

3. With the heat still on medium-low, place the bun in the skillet, cut-side down. Push it around to coat it lightly with the butter and toast it until golden, 1 minute.

4. Place the bun on a serving plate and top with the shrimp mixture. Top with 2 or 3 dashes of hot sauce (if using) and enjoy.

Ingredient Tip: You can use frozen uncooked shrimp if you have that on hand. Place the frozen shrimp directly in the skillet and cook over medium heat until pink, stirring occasionally. Drain and wipe the skillet before proceeding with the recipe.

Use It Up: Leftover corn can be used for Coconut-Corn Chowder (page 46) and celery for Chicken and Rice Noodle Soup (page 55). Have leftover crab from Crab Cakes with Lemon Cream (page 83)? Heat it in the butter along with the shrimp.

STUFFED CHEDDAR BURGER WITH CHARRED RED ONION AND SPECIAL SAUCE

PREP TIME: 10 MINUTES / COOK TIME: 15 MINUTES

Ever heard of a "Juicy Lucy"? It's a burger stuffed with cheese in the middle rather than on top and is said to have originated in a Minnesota bar. Sounds delicious, right? You can use just about any cheese you want for stuffing—blue or smoked provolone—but we're going classic with this recipe, which calls for cheddar. A tangy special sauce balances it all out, but feel free to add toppings such as lettuce, tomato, or pickles.

½ teaspoon salt

½ teaspoon freshly ground black pepper

¼ teaspoon garlic powder

¼ teaspoon onion powder

½ pound ground beef (⁸⁰⁄₂₀)

2 slices cheddar quartered

1 tablespoon ketchup

1 teaspoon Worcestershire sauce

2 bread-and-butter pickle slices, chopped, plus more for garnish

1 red onion ring, about ¼-inch thick

1 tablespoon unsalted butter

1 teaspoon avocado or other high-heat oil

1 brioche hamburger bun, lightly toasted

1 to 2 leaves butter or romaine lettuce (optional)

1. Combine the salt, pepper, garlic powder, and onion powder in a medium bowl. Add the beef and mix it into the seasoning. Gently shape half the beef into a patty. Place it on a plate or baking sheet, lightly pressing down to flatten it so it is thin. Repeat with the remaining beef.

2. Top one patty with the cheese in the center, leaving a ½- to 1-inch border. Place the other patty on top and pinch the edges to seal.

3. In a small bowl, combine the ketchup, Worcestershire sauce, and pickles, stirring to combine. Set aside.

4. Heat a cast-iron skillet or pan over medium-high heat. When hot, add the onion ring and press down with a metal spatula to char it, holding for about 1 minute. Flip and repeat on the other side until it is charred and softened, 1 minute more. Transfer to a plate and set aside.

5. Reduce the heat to medium and add the butter and oil. When it's sizzling, add the burger patty. Sear it until it's brown, 2 minutes. Carefully flip and sear 2 minutes longer. Cover with a fitted lid or small saucepan (to prevent pushing down on the burger) and cook until the cheese melts, 5 minutes, or until the temperature of the beef reaches 160°F. Transfer the burger to the plate with the onion and let it rest for 2 minutes.

6. Meanwhile, spread the bottom and top halves of the bun evenly with the sauce. Place the burger on the bottom bun, top with the onion, lettuce, and more pickles (if using). Close with the top bun and enjoy immediately.

Ingredient Tip: To cut the onion, slice a thin piece off the top and discard. Slice a ½-inch thick ring, peeling and discarding the skin. You can dice the rest of the onion and store it in the refrigerator or freezer, make quick-pickled red onions (see Fish Tacos, page 38), thinly slice and use it for Tangy Onion Soup with Cheese Toast (page 56), or leave the rest of the skin and bulb intact, cover, and store in a dark, cool place for 1 more day before transferring to the refrigerator.

Use It Up: You can use leftover pickles for the Sticky Rice Bowl with Pickled Carrots, Cucumbers, and Fried Egg (page 70) as a shortcut.

FISH TACOS WITH QUICK-PICKLED RED ONIONS AND SMOKY CHILI CREAM

PREP TIME: 15 MINUTES / COOK TIME: 15 MINUTES

Fresh fish tacos always remind me of sunny California or trips to Mexico, but they can seem intimidating to make at home. I'm here to prove they don't have to be! This simple recipe will have you feeling beachy in no time—no frying or grill needed thanks to the smokiness of the chili powder.

1 (6-ounce) fillet flaky fish (whitefish, halibut, cod, tilapia), cut into 1-inch-wide pieces

1 teaspoon extra-virgin olive (or other neutral) oil

⅛ teaspoon salt

⅛ teaspoon freshly ground black pepper

¼ teaspoon ground cumin

¾ teaspoon chili powder, divided

1 small lime

½ red onion, diced

Apple cider vinegar

¼ cup sour cream (or plain Greek yogurt)

3 corn tortillas

¼ cup coleslaw mix or thinly sliced Napa cabbage

Chopped fresh cilantro, for garnish (optional)

Crumbled cotija cheese, for garnish (optional)

1. Preheat the oven to 425°F.

2. Place the fish in an 8-inch glass baking dish. Brush the fish with the olive oil and season with the salt and pepper. Sprinkle the cumin and ¼ teaspoon chili powder evenly over the fish.

3. Zest half of the lime and place in a small bowl. Set aside. Cut the lime in half, and then cut one half into 2 wedges. Set aside. Squeeze the other half evenly over the fish, taking care not to let the seeds fall onto the fish. Let the fish "marinate" while you make the onions.

4. In a small bowl (or jar), combine the onion and enough apple cider vinegar to cover. Give the mixture a quick stir or shake and refrigerate.

5. Bake the fish until it is cooked through and opaque in the middle, 15 minutes.

6. Meanwhile, in the bowl with the lime zest, mix together the sour cream and remaining ½ teaspoon of chili powder.

7. To serve, remove the fish from the oven and flake with a fork. Spread each tortilla with a couple tablespoons of chili cream. Top evenly with the fish and coleslaw mix, and 1 tablespoon of red onion. Top with cilantro and cotija, if using. Serve with lime wedges.

Use It Up: Leftover coleslaw or cabbage can be used for Chicken Tenders with Tonkatsu and Coleslaw (page 105).

GINGER CHICKEN AND CHILE LETTUCE WRAPS

PREP TIME: 15 MINUTES / COOK TIME: 10 MINUTES

Decades after this classic was "invented" by a popular Asian-inspired chain restaurant, I still can't get enough of it and enjoy any and all variations. This version features chopped jalapeño peppers for some heat, along with plenty of refreshing ginger, lime, and cilantro.

4 to 6 ounces ground chicken

⅛ teaspoon salt

¼ teaspoon freshly ground black pepper

2 tablespoons sesame oil, divided

1 tablespoon soy sauce

1 scallion, thinly sliced, green and white parts separated

1 tablespoon minced fresh ginger

1 garlic clove, minced

1 small jalapeño, seeded, membrane removed, finely chopped

1 small carrot

Juice of 1 lime

¼ cup chopped fresh cilantro

4 large butterhead lettuce leaves

Toasted sesame seeds, for garnish (optional)

1. Season the chicken with the salt and pepper. Set aside.

2. Heat 1 tablespoon of oil in a skillet over medium heat. Cook the chicken until it is brown and cooked through, stirring frequently to break up the meat, 5 minutes.

3. Using a slotted spoon, transfer the cooked chicken to a medium bowl. Add the soy sauce and stir to combine.

4. Add the remaining 1 tablespoon of oil and the white scallion parts and cook over medium heat until soft, 2 minutes. Add the ginger, garlic, and jalapeño and cook until fragrant, 30 seconds. Spoon into the bowl with the chicken. Peel the carrot into thin strips, discarding the outer layer and putting the rest over the chicken. Add the scallion green parts, lime juice, and cilantro, tossing to combine.

5. Place the lettuce leaves on a serving plate, cup-side up. Divide the chicken mixture evenly among the lettuce cups. Top with the sesame seeds (if using), roll up, and enjoy.

Ingredient Tip: To best use and preserve butterhead lettuce, remove the leaves by tearing just above the bulb, keeping bulb intact. Wrap them in a paper towel and place in a resealable plastic bag in the refrigerator.

Use It Up: Swap the turkey in Turkey Meatball Soup with Swiss Chard and Dill (page 51) to use up this batch of ground chicken. You could also use any leftover ground pork from Pork Noodles with Chili Oil (page 98) instead of the chicken here.

SWEET AND SAVORY SLOPPY JOES WITH SPICED PICKLES

PREP TIME: 10 MINUTES / COOK TIME: 15 MINUTES

Cooking sloppy joes with pear adds sweetness, similar to the Korean method of sweetening bulgogi, a beef dish. The gentle spice of the pickles rounds out the flavors. You can always use store-bought pickles or make an extra batch for use in other dishes.

FOR THE PICKLES

½ seedless English cucumber or 2 small Persian cucumbers, cut into ¼-inch-thick pieces

2 tablespoons rice wine vinegar

½ tablespoon red pepper flakes

2 teaspoons maple syrup

¼ teaspoon salt

1 teaspoon toasted sesame seed oil

FOR THE SLOPPY JOES

1 small Bosc pear, peeled

½ yellow onion, peeled

1 garlic clove, peeled

1 (2-inch) piece ginger, peeled

1 tablespoon avocado oil

¼ to ⅓ pound ground beef

¼ teaspoon freshly ground black pepper

3 tablespoons tomato paste

1 tablespoon soy sauce

1 tablespoon Worcestershire sauce

¼ cup beef or chicken stock

1 brioche hamburger bun, lightly toasted

Toasted sesame seeds, for garnish (optional)

TO MAKE THE PICKLES

1. Toss together the cucumber, vinegar, red pepper flakes, maple syrup, salt, and oil in a small bowl. Cover and refrigerate.

TO MAKE THE SLOPPY JOES

2. Grate the pear, onion, garlic, and ginger into a bowl. Set aside.

3. Heat the oil in a medium deep skillet over medium-high heat. Add the beef and cook until it is brown, 3 to 4 minutes. Season with the pepper.

4. Add the pear mixture, stirring to combine. Add the tomato paste, soy sauce, Worcestershire sauce, and stock. Cover and bring almost to a boil. Reduce the heat and simmer, uncovered, until the liquid has evaporated and the grated ingredients have softened, 10 minutes.

5. To serve, drain the pickles. Pile the bottom bun with the pickles. Top with the meat mixture and sesame seeds (if using). Close with the top bun and enjoy warm.

Make It Faster: Use your favorite bread-and-butter or other thin sliced jarred pickles and add a few red pepper flakes to spice them up, if desired.

Use It Up: Instead of ground beef, you can use leftover ground pork from Pork Noodles with Chili Oil (page 98) or a combination of ground beef and pork—whatever you have on hand.

FLATBREAD WITH PROSCIUTTO, GOAT CHEESE, AND BROCCOLI

PREP TIME: 10 MINUTES / COOK TIME: 20 MINUTES

This is a light and lovely pizza option, and it is a fun appetizer for guests. The balsamic-soaked shallot brightens up the richness of the goat cheese and pairs well with the prosciutto and broccoli (see the tip for making a glaze). When purchasing prepared pizza dough, separate it into quarters and freeze them individually for longer-term storage.

1 small shallot, thinly sliced

2 tablespoons balsamic vinegar

1 ounce goat cheese

¼ cup cream cheese

½ cup broccoli florets

¼ prepared pizza dough, or 1 whole naan bread

1 teaspoon extra-virgin olive oil, plus more for garnish

2 ounces prosciutto

Freshly ground black pepper

1. Combine the shallot and vinegar in a small bowl. Set aside. Mix together the goat and cream cheese in a separate small bowl. Set them aside to soften.
2. Place a pizza pan or rimmed baking sheet in the oven and preheat to 450°F.
3. Fill a small saucepan with 1 inch of water and bring to a simmer. Add the broccoli; cover and steam until it is bright green and tender, about 2 minutes. Drain or remove the broccoli with a slotted spoon and set aside.
4. Roll out the pizza dough on a lightly floured surface. Remove the preheated pan from the oven. Place the pizza dough in the center of the pan, spreading it out to thin it, and brush it lightly with the olive oil. Spread the cheese mixture evenly over the dough, leaving a 1-inch border. Top evenly with the drained shallots and the broccoli and then the prosciutto.
5. Return the pan to the oven and bake until the broccoli is slightly charred and the dough is golden brown, 12 to 15 minutes. Season with pepper, and if desired, more olive oil and balsamic vinegar. Cut into 4-inch squares or fold in half and enjoy as a handheld.

Ingredient Tip: A balsamic glaze goes well with this flatbread. You can use your microwave to make it: microwave the vinegar in a small microwave-safe bowl on 50 percent power for 60 to 90 seconds, taking care not to burn it. Immediately drizzle it over the pizza.

TUNA NIÇOISE SALAD PITA POCKETS WITH SOFT-BOILED EGGS

IN A PINCH / PREP TIME: 10 MINUTES / COOK TIME: 10 MINUTES

The classic version of this salad calls for hard-boiled eggs, but soft-boiled are so decadent, and you can make extra and store them in the refrigerator to top Avocado Toast with Balsamic and Black Pepper (page 18) or Sticky Rice Bowl with Pickled Carrots, Cucumbers, and Fried Egg (page 70). To save time, we're skipping the potatoes (unless you have some cooked ones on hand) and stuffing the salad into a pita pocket for a handheld option.

1 large egg

1 cup trimmed, halved green beans

2 tablespoons extra-virgin olive oil

Juice from 1 small lemon

2 teaspoons Dijon mustard

¼ teaspoon freshly ground black pepper

1 (4- to 5-ounce) can tuna, drained

4 cherry or grape tomatoes, quartered

¼ cup pitted black olives, thinly sliced

2 butter or romaine lettuce leaves

1 piece pita bread, warmed, halved

1. Bring a small saucepan of water to boil. Carefully drop in the egg using a slotted spoon. Turn off the heat, cover, and let sit for 8 minutes. Use the slotted spoon to transfer the egg to a small bowl filled with ice and water and chill until just slightly warm, 2 minutes. If you made more eggs, chill the extras completely before refrigerating them.

2. Meanwhile, in a microwave-safe bowl filled with an inch of water, cook the beans, covered loosely, at 50 percent power until the beans are tender, 2 minutes. Drain and cool. Pat dry.

3. In a medium bowl, whisk together the olive oil, lemon juice, Dijon mustard, and pepper. Flake the tuna into the bowl and add the green beans, tomatoes, and olives. Toss to combine. Line each pita half with 1 small piece of lettuce and stuff evenly with the tuna mixture.

4. Gently crack and peel the egg. Cut the egg in quarters over the pita to catch any still-runny egg yolk and tuck two pieces into each pita half. Enjoy immediately. (The pitas can be wrapped, chilled, and enjoyed later or the next day, but skip the lettuce so they don't get soggy.)

Make It Faster: Use leftover green beans from Halibut and Green Beans with Chermoula (page 91).

CHAPTER 4

Soups and Stews

< Curried Lentil and Butternut Squash Soup,
  page 54

COCONUT-CORN CHOWDER

IN A PINCH / PREP TIME: 5 MINUTES / COOK TIME: 15 MINUTES / MAKES ABOUT 2 CUPS

I love this super-easy soup for a fast lunch or light dinner when I'm low on groceries and need to rely on the pantry. A little lime zest, garlic, and shallot round everything out with brightness and aromatics.

1 tablespoon coconut oil
or butter

1 small shallot, thinly sliced
(about 2 tablespoons)

1 garlic clove, minced

1 cup corn kernels, frozen or
canned and drained

1 (14.5-ounce) can
coconut milk

Zest and juice of ½ lime

1. Melt the oil in a medium saucepan over medium heat. Add the shallot and garlic and cook until soft and fragrant, 2 minutes.

2. Add the corn. Pour in the coconut milk. Cover and bring to a simmer. Simmer until the corn is tender and the flavors meld, 8 to 10 minutes.

3. Stir in the lime zest and juice and enjoy.

Ingredient Tip: Add chopped precooked shrimp, cooked crabmeat, or shredded chicken for extra protein. You could also top the soup with a little queso fresco and chopped fresh cilantro and/or thin, green scallion slices, if desired. Or, even better, use crunchy chickpeas from Crunchy Chickpea and Tahini Caesar Salad (page 33).

GREEN CHICKEN CHILI WITH AVOCADO AND TOASTED PUMPKIN SEEDS

PREP TIME: 10 MINUTES / COOK TIME: 15 MINUTES / MAKES ABOUT 2 CUPS

If you have a jar of good quality, "clean label" green salsa (meaning limited, all-natural ingredients with no additives, preservatives, or added oils) and a boneless chicken breast (or thighs), you're good to go for this quick and easy soup. Pumpkin seeds add a nice crunch and toasty flavor.

2 tablespoons pumpkin seeds (pepitas)

1 boneless, skinless chicken breast, cut into 1-inch cubes

1½ cups store-bought mild green salsa

¼ cup chicken broth or stock

¼ cup cubed avocado, for garnish (optional)

Chopped fresh cilantro, for garnish (optional)

Sour cream, for garnish (optional)

1. Heat a medium saucepan over medium heat. Add the pumpkin seeds and toast them, stirring constantly, until fragrant, 1 to 2 minutes. Pour them out onto a plate and spread them out to cool. Set aside.

2. In the same saucepan, combine the chicken, salsa, and broth. Cover and bring to a boil. Reduce the heat to a simmer and cook until the chicken is cooked through, 10 minutes.

3. Ladle the soup into a large soup bowl. Top with the pumpkin seeds. Garnish with avocado, cilantro, and sour cream (if using).

Make It Faster: Use precooked chicken breast, cut into cubes.

EGG DROP RAMEN WITH SCALLIONS AND SESAME

IN A PINCH / PREP TIME: 5 MINUTES / COOK TIME: 10 MINUTES / MAKES ABOUT 1½ CUPS

When I was very young and we lived in the city, my mom often took me to the local diner, where I always got the lemon egg drop soup. It's such a simple soup but so satisfying and comforting. Now that I'm older and appreciate a wider range of global flavors, I've developed this egg drop soup to include soy and scallions with noodles for a make-your-own ramen-style bowl of joy.

1 cup chicken broth

1 to 2 ounces udon or rice noodles

1 large egg

Zest and juice of 1 small lemon

⅛ teaspoon freshly ground black pepper

1 teaspoon soy sauce

1 small scallion, thinly sliced (green parts only), for garnish

1 to 2 teaspoons sesame seeds, for garnish

1. Bring the broth to a boil in a medium saucepan over medium heat. Add the noodles, reduce the heat, and simmer until cooked through, 5 minutes.

2. Turn off the heat. Using tongs, transfer the noodles to a large soup bowl.

3. In a small bowl, crack the egg and whisk with the lemon juice and pepper. Slowly whisk in 1 cup of hot broth to temper the egg and prevent curdling.

4. Pour the egg mixture into the broth in the saucepan, stirring continually in the same direction.

5. Immediately pour the broth over the noodles. Stir in the lemon zest and soy sauce, garnish with scallion and sesame seeds, and enjoy.

VERY TOMATOEY SOUP WITH PARMESAN CRISP

PREP TIME: 10 MINUTES / COOK TIME: 15 MINUTES / MAKES ABOUT 2 CUPS

Nothing beats a comforting tomato soup (and maybe a little bread and cheese) on a cold day or when you need a food hug. This soup is super easy to make, and you can play around with the ingredients: If you like a creamy soup, blend everything before enjoying or leave the chunks for a heartier meal. You could even add a little diced carrot if you want extra veg.

¼ cup grated
Parmesan cheese

2 tablespoons unsalted butter

½ small yellow onion, diced

2 tablespoons balsamic or red wine vinegar

1 (8-ounce) can crushed tomatoes or tomato sauce

1 (8-ounce) can tomato juice

½ teaspoon dried oregano

½ teaspoon freshly ground black pepper

Pinch salt

1 heaping tablespoon sour cream (optional)

Torn basil leaves, for garnish

1. To make the Parmesan crisp, heat a saucepan over medium heat. Pile the cheese in the center and flatten lightly with a spatula. Cook until the cheese is melted and light brown, 3 minutes. Turn off the heat and cool slightly. Use the spatula to transfer to a plate to cool completely.

2. Melt the butter in the same saucepan over medium heat. Add the onion and cook until it begins to caramelize, 5 minutes. Add the vinegar and cook until the liquid evaporates, scraping up the browned bits.

3. Stir in the tomatoes, tomato juice, oregano, pepper, and salt. Cover and bring to a light simmer. Cook the mixture until it is warm and the onions are super soft, 3 to 5 minutes.

4. Transfer the mixture to a blender. Process until it is smooth and creamy.

5. Ladle the soup into a bowl. Top with sour cream (if using), the basil, and the Parmesan crisp.

Ingredient Tip: If you have leftover fresh mozzarella from Marinated Vegetable Salad with Fresh Mozzarella (page 31), you can skip the Parmesan crisp and just put a few torn mozzarella pieces in the bottom of the soup bowl before ladling in the soup.

EASY BROCCOLI-CHEESE SOUP

PREP TIME: 10 MINUTES / COOK TIME: 15 MINUTES / MAKES ABOUT 2 CUPS

I'm not a huge fan of flour in soup—there's something about the metallic taste and consistency I don't love—so I developed this recipe thickened with cannellini beans, which are super creamy when cooked down, and a touch of sour cream added at the end. The more cheese you add, the thicker your soup will turn out! Croutons add a nice crunch.

1 teaspoon unsalted butter

1 garlic clove, minced

1 teaspoon apple cider vinegar

2 cups fresh or frozen broccoli florets, coarsely chopped

⅓ cup cannellini beans, drained, rinsed

1½ cups chicken or vegetable broth or stock

1 cup shredded cheddar cheese, plus more if desired

Freshly ground black pepper

Sour cream, for garnish

1. Melt the butter in a medium saucepan over medium heat. Add the garlic and cook until fragrant, 1 minute. Add the vinegar and cook until evaporated, 1 minute.

2. Add the broccoli, beans, and broth. Cover and bring to a boil. Reduce the heat and simmer until the broccoli is tender, 10 minutes.

3. Pour the soup into a blender (or use an immersion blender) and blend until smooth, with bits of broccoli still visible.

4. While it is still hot, pour the soup into a bowl. Add the cheese, a pinch at a time, stirring constantly to melt. Garnish with pepper and a dollop of sour cream and enjoy.

Use It Up: Leftover cannellini beans can be used for Pan-Fried Pork Chop with Creamy Beans and Greens (page 106). Use extra broccoli for Flatbread with Prosciutto, Goat Cheese, and Broccoli (page 42).

TURKEY MEATBALL SOUP WITH SWISS CHARD AND DILL

PREP TIME: 10 MINUTES / COOK TIME: 20 MINUTES / MAKES 8 MEATBALLS

This soup reminds me of Italian wedding soup, which is made with sausage-based meatballs, but it's lighter overall because of the ground turkey, and the dill softens the flavors. The red pepper in the meatballs adds a little pop of color, flavor, and nutrition.

½ pound ground turkey, no more than 90 percent lean

4 jarred roasted red peppers, drained, finely chopped

1 bread slice, torn into very small pieces, or ¼ cup panko

1 tablespoon chopped fresh parsley

1 tablespoon grated Parmesan cheese

½ tablespoon garlic powder

½ tablespoon onion powder

¼ teaspoon salt

¼ teaspoon freshly ground black pepper

1 large egg

1 teaspoon avocado or other high-heat oil

2 cups low-sodium chicken broth or stock

3 leaves Swiss chard, torn into small pieces

2 tablespoons chopped fresh dill

1. Combine the turkey, peppers, bread, parsley, Parmesan, garlic powder, onion powder, salt, and pepper in a large bowl. Crack the egg into the bowl and gently mix to combine, without overmixing.
2. Shape into 2-inch meatballs.
3. Heat the oil in a medium saucepan or Dutch oven over medium-high heat. Add the meatballs and cook until they are brown on all sides, 4 minutes. Turn them occasionally.
4. Pour in the broth, cover, and bring to a simmer. Simmer until the meatballs are cooked through and their internal temperature reads 165°F, 20 minutes.
5. In the last few minutes of cooking, stir in the chard and dill, cover, and cook until wilted. To serve, ladle into a large soup bowl and enjoy.

Use It Up: The recipe for the meatballs in this soup is the same as Turkey and Roasted Red Pepper Meatballs (page 109). I recommend making this whole batch and using 2 to 4 meatballs for this soup and the rest for the main dish. They will last in the refrigerator a day or two or can be frozen for later use.

SEAFOOD STEW WITH FENNEL AND ROUILLE TOAST

PREP TIME: 10 MINUTES / COOK TIME: 20 MINUTES / MAKES 2 CUPS

Rouille is a Provençale sauce typically made from red pepper flakes and water-soaked, blended bread crumbs and is often served with bouillabaisse. For a deconstructed rendition, this recipe uses a quick roasted red pepper blend (or you can use the romesco sauce from page 100) that you can spread on crusty bread and partially soak in the stew to soften.

FOR THE STEW

1 tablespoon extra-virgin olive oil

1 shallot, thinly sliced

½ small fennel bulb, thinly sliced

1 garlic clove, chopped fine

1 heaping tablespoon tomato paste

1 teaspoon red wine vinegar

1 (6.5-ounce) can clams plus juices

2 ounces frozen or fresh peeled and deveined shrimp

½ cup canned whole tomatoes plus juices

¼ cup water or stock

Chopped fresh fennel fronds, parsley, or torn basil leaves, for garnish (optional)

FOR THE ROUILLE TOAST

1 piece crusty bread or oblong slice of baguette

1 garlic clove

4 jarred roasted red peppers, drained

¼ teaspoon red pepper flakes

1 tablespoon extra-virgin olive oil

TO MAKE THE STEW

1. Heat the olive oil in a medium saucepan over medium heat. Add the shallot and fennel and cook until soft and fragrant, 5 minutes. Add the garlic and tomato paste and let caramelize while stirring the garlic, 30 seconds. Stir in the vinegar and cook until the liquid evaporates, scraping up the browned bits.

2. Add the clams and shrimp. Crush the tomatoes in your hands over the pot, allowing the juices to fall in. Add the water, cover, and bring to a simmer. Cook until the shrimp is pink, 5 to 7 minutes.

TO MAKE THE ROUILLE TOAST

3. Rub the bread with the garlic clove. Toast in a toaster oven or 350°F oven until golden. Add the garlic to the bowl of a food processor with the red peppers, red pepper flakes, and olive oil. Pulse until smooth. Spread the sauce on the toast. Set aside.

4. Ladle the stew into a large serving bowl. Top with herbs (if using), and nestle the rouille toast into the stew. Enjoy.

Ingredient Tip: I love the delicate flavor of fennel in this soup, but you could use celery for quicker cooking or even omit it altogether.

CURRIED LENTIL AND BUTTERNUT SQUASH SOUP

GOOD FOR SCALING / PREP TIME: 5 MINUTES / COOK TIME: 20 MINUTES / MAKES 2 CUPS

This soup is great for a light and healthy lunch. You can also make a bigger batch and freeze it for quick go-to meals. Using precut frozen butternut squash makes prep work much easier, and for more veggies, stir in some baby spinach at the end of the cooking time.

1 tablespoon coconut oil

¼ cup chopped yellow onion

½ teaspoon curry powder

½ teaspoon turmeric

¼ teaspoon ground cumin

¼ teaspoon salt

¼ teaspoon freshly ground black pepper

1 garlic clove, minced

1 tablespoon tomato paste

2 cups chopped frozen butternut squash

¼ cup dried red lentils

1½ cup chicken or vegetable stock

1 lime wedge

1 heaping tablespoon plain Greek yogurt, for garnish (optional)

Chopped fresh cilantro or basil, for garnish (optional)

Toasted pepitas or nuts, for garnish (optional)

1. Melt the oil in a medium saucepan over medium heat. Add the onion, curry powder, turmeric, cumin, salt, and pepper and cook until soft and translucent, 2 minutes.

2. Add the garlic and cook until fragrant, 30 seconds. Add the tomato paste and let caramelize, 30 seconds. Stir and add the squash, lentils, and stock. Cover and bring to a simmer.

3. Simmer until the lentils are cooked through and the squash is tender, 15 minutes. Transfer the mixture to a blender and blend until smooth if you prefer a creamier texture.

4. Serve with a lime wedge and yogurt, cilantro or basil, and pepitas (if using).

Ingredient Tip: For extra crunch, top with crunchy chickpeas (see Crunchy Chickpea and Tahini Caesar Salad, page 33), homemade croutons (leftover bread, cubed, coated with oil, and toasted), or chopped nuts of your choice.

CHICKEN AND RICE NOODLE SOUP

PREP TIME: 10 MINUTES / COOK TIME: 20 MINUTES / MAKES ABOUT 3 CUPS

I always love a good chicken soup; this version has a twist with some mushrooms, lime juice, soy sauce, and scallions for a pop of flavor. (I often top this soup with peanuts or cashews for crunch, too.) Rice noodles take just seconds to cook, but you could use any pasta or noodle that you prefer; just adjust the simmering time.

1 tablespoon unsalted butter

1 scallion, chopped, green and white parts separated

½ cup chopped mushrooms

¼ cup chopped carrots

1 garlic clove, minced

½ teaspoon minced fresh ginger

1 boneless, skinless chicken breast

2¼ cups low-sodium chicken broth or chicken stock

1 tablespoon soy sauce

Juice of 1 lime

¼ teaspoon kosher salt

⅛ teaspoon freshly ground black pepper

2 ounces dry rice noodles

2 teaspoons chopped fresh parsley or cilantro, for garnish (optional)

1. Melt the butter in a medium saucepan over medium heat. Add the white parts of the scallion, mushrooms, and carrots and cook until the vegetables begin to soften, 3 minutes. Stir in the garlic and ginger and cook until fragrant, 30 seconds.

2. Add the chicken, stock, soy sauce, lime juice, salt (if using unsalted stock), and pepper. Cover and bring to a simmer. Simmer until the chicken is cooked through and easily shreds with a fork, 20 minutes.

3. Transfer the chicken to a chopping board. Add the noodles to the pan, cover, and simmer until cooked through, 3 minutes. While the noodles are cooking, shred the chicken using two forks.

4. Place the chicken in a large soup bowl. Pour the soup on top. Top with herbs (if using) and enjoy.

Ingredient Tip: Substitute noodles for leftover gnocchi, if you have it on hand from Sheet Pan Gnocchi with Blistered Tomatoes and Broccoli Rabe (page 64), or you can add orzo from Lemony Tuna with Orzo, Dill, and Cucumber (page 79).

Make It Faster: Use shredded precooked or rotisserie chicken.

TANGY ONION SOUP WITH CHEESE TOAST

PREP TIME: 10 MINUTES / COOK TIME: 20 MINUTES / MAKES 2 CUPS

My mom loves fresh-baked croissants and French onion soup. When I was little, she would often take us to a local French café where I would enjoy both wholeheartedly. Now, I can be found in the kitchen stirring and caramelizing onions for just about anything, including this comforting soup. This quicker-cooking version skips the broiler process, but don't forget to nestle the bread in the soup to soften as you slurp.

2 tablespoons unsalted butter

1 small yellow onion, thinly sliced

¼ cup sherry vinegar (or apple cider or red wine vinegar)

½ teaspoon dried thyme

Pinch salt

¼ teaspoon coarsely ground black pepper

1½ cups low-sodium beef broth

1 thick slice French or other crusty bread

1 garlic clove

¼ cup shredded Gruyère cheese

2 teaspoons chopped fresh parsley (optional)

1. Melt the butter in a medium saucepan over medium heat. Add the onion and cook until very soft and caramelized, 15 minutes.

2. Add the vinegar and cook until most of the liquid has evaporated, 2 minutes.

3. Add the thyme, salt, pepper, and broth. Cover and bring to a simmer. Cook until it is warmed through and the flavors have melded, 5 minutes.

4. While the soup simmers, place the bread on a rimmed baking sheet lined with aluminum foil. Rub with the garlic and top with the cheese. Toast in the toaster oven or in a 350°F oven until the cheese melts and bubbles.

5. Ladle the soup into a large bowl. Top with the cheese toast and parsley (if using). Enjoy.

Use It Up: Have leftover broth? Pour it into ice cube trays or into resealable plastic bags with the air pushed out, lay it flat on a tray or plate, and place it in the freezer. When frozen, remove the tray or plate. Freezing liquids this way saves freezer space.

SMOKY HAM POSOLE WITH POBLANO

PREP TIME: 10 MINUTES / COOK TIME: 20 MINUTES / MAKES ABOUT 2 CUPS

1 poblano pepper

1 tablespoon unsalted butter

1 small shallot, thinly sliced

1 garlic clove, minced

1¼ cups cubed, precooked ham steak

½ teaspoon chili powder

2 cups chicken broth or stock

1 cup canned, cooked hominy, drained, rinsed

Juice of ½ lime

Chopped fresh cilantro, for garnish (optional)

Tortilla chips or strips, for garnish (optional)

Crumbed queso fresco or shredded cheddar cheese, for garnish (optional)

Thinly sliced radish, for garnish (optional)

Hot sauce (optional)

1. Turn on a burner to medium-low. Using heatproof tongs, hold the pepper over the flame (or on top of an electric plate), flipping it every 5 to 10 seconds, until it is charred in places and fragrant, 2 minutes. Watch closely in case of flare-ups. Set aside and cool slightly. When the pepper is cool enough to handle, coarsely chop the poblano.

2. Melt the butter in a medium saucepan over medium-low heat. Add the shallot, garlic, and ham until the mixture is fragrant and beginning to soften, 3 minutes.

3. Stir in the chili powder. Add the broth and hominy. Cover and bring to a boil. Reduce the heat and simmer until the flavors meld and the poblano is tender, 15 minutes.

4. Ladle the soup into a large bowl. Stir in the lime juice, top with cilantro, tortilla chips, cheese, radish, and hot sauce, if using, and enjoy.

Use It Up: Add hominy to Ratatouille Pasta with Torn Basil (page 69) instead of the pasta, or toast in a 450°F oven and use as a crunchy topper for other soups, salads, or as a snack. Add any extra ham to Pepper and Egg Muffin Cups (page 23).

BEEF AND BEAN CHILI

PREP TIME: 10 MINUTES / COOK TIME: 20 MINUTES / MAKES ABOUT 2 CUPS

This chili is pretty easy to make and uses several ingredients you might already have on hand (feel free to substitute black or pinto beans for red kidney beans, if you have those instead). You can even use this recipe for an easy and delicious taco filling; just drain the tomatoes first and cook uncovered to allow the juices to evaporate.

2 teaspoons extra-virgin olive oil

½ cup chopped yellow onion

1 garlic clove, minced

1 small serrano or ½ jalapeño, seeded, membrane removed, finely chopped

3 ounces ground beef

¼ teaspoon kosher salt

¼ teaspoon chili powder

¼ teaspoon ground cumin

¼ cup canned red kidney beans, rinsed, drained

1 (15-ounce) can diced tomatoes, including juice

Chopped fresh cilantro, for garnish (optional)

Sour cream, for garnish (optional)

Shredded cheddar cheese, for garnish (optional)

Diced avocado, for garnish (optional)

Lime wedge, for garnish (optional)

1. Heat the olive oil in a 4-quart saucepan or deep skillet with a lid. Add the onion and cook until soft and translucent, stirring occasionally, 2 minutes. Stir in the garlic and serrano and cook until fragrant, 30 seconds.

2. Add the beef to the skillet and cook until no longer pink, breaking it up with a spoon, 5 minutes.

3. Stir in the salt, chili powder, and cumin. Add the beans and tomatoes. Cover and bring to a boil. Reduce the heat and simmer until the flavors meld, 10 minutes.

4. Ladle the chili into a large bowl, top with the cilantro, sour cream, cheese, avocado, and lime, if using, and enjoy.

CHAPTER 5

Vegetable Mains

< Red Lentil and Tomato Dal, page 68

STUFFED PEPPERS WITH SPICED BEANS, QUINOA, AND CILANTRO CREAM

GOOD FOR SCALING / PREP TIME: 10 MINUTES / COOK TIME: 20 MINUTES

This easy-to-make, hearty recipe offers plenty of options and can be scaled to feed more. You can use any type of bean you have on hand, and any other shredded cheese, such as Monterey Jack or queso fresco. Or, omit it altogether if preferred.

1 red, yellow, or orange
bell pepper

¼ cup dry quinoa

1 tablespoon extra-virgin
olive oil

1 small shallot, finely chopped

1 garlic clove, minced

¾ cup unsalted or low-salt
vegetable broth (or
filtered water)

2 teaspoons ground cumin

2 teaspoons chili powder

⅓ cup canned tri-bean blend,
rinsed and drained

½ cup shredded cheddar
cheese, divided

1 small serrano pepper,
seeded, membranes removed,
and finely chopped

3 tablespoons sour cream

1 tablespoon chopped cilantro
leaves, for garnish (optional)

Zest and juice of ½ lime

1. Preheat the oven or toaster oven to 350°F.

2. Slice off the top of the pepper and remove the seeds and membranes. Trim the bottom so it can stand upright. Place the pepper, cut-side up, on a small baking sheet lined with aluminum foil or in a small glass baking dish.

3. Coarsely chop the remaining pepper trimmed from the top and bottom, discarding the stem, and set aside. Place the pepper in the oven while preparing the stuffing.

4. Heat a medium saucepan over medium heat. Pour in the quinoa and toast until fragrant, 30 seconds. Add the olive oil, shallot, and reserved bell pepper, cooking until softened, 2 minutes. Add the garlic and cook until fragrant, 30 seconds. Stir in the broth, cumin, and chili powder. Cover, bring to a boil, and reduce the heat to medium-low. Simmer until all the liquid has been absorbed, 15 minutes. Turn off the heat and fold in the beans, half the cheese, and the serrano.

5. Remove the pepper from the oven and stuff it with the bean mixture. Sprinkle the remaining cheese on top and bake until the cheese melts, 2 minutes.

6. Meanwhile, mix the sour cream, cilantro (if using), and lime zest and juice. Transfer the pepper to a plate and drizzle with the cream mixture. Enjoy immediately.

Make It Faster: Skip the cilantro cream and just squeeze a lime wedge over the pepper and top with chopped cilantro.

TOFU AND SNOW PEA STIR-FRY WITH SOBA NOODLES

PREP TIME: 10 MINUTES / COOK TIME: 20 MINUTES

Many stir-fry dishes use cornstarch as a thickener for sauces. To avoid having to purchase a big batch of cornstarch, or just to omit it from your diet, this recipe uses a touch of maple syrup and Dijon mustard as both thickening and flavoring agents. Just be sure that the sauce has cooled a bit before adding the mustard, or it can break up the sauce. Cashews add a nice crunch to the dish.

14 ounces firm or extra-firm tofu, drained

Salt

Freshly ground black pepper

2 tablespoons avocado or other high-heat oil, divided

1 cup snow peas

1 small red serrano, seeded and membranes removed

1 scallion, thinly sliced, white and green parts separated

2 teaspoons minced ginger

1 garlic clove, minced

1 tablespoon soy sauce

1 tablespoon rice vinegar

1 teaspoon maple syrup or honey

1 teaspoon Dijon mustard

1 cup cooked soba noodles, warmed in the microwave

Roasted, chopped unsalted or lightly salted cashews

1. Squeeze excess moisture out of the tofu using paper towels and season it with the salt and pepper.

2. In a medium skillet over medium-high heat, heat 1 tablespoon of oil until shimmering. Add the tofu and sear it until it is golden brown on both sides, turning once, 6 minutes. Transfer the tofu to a serving bowl and set aside.

3. Add 1 tablespoon of oil to the pan, and add the snow peas, serrano, and scallion white parts. Cook, stirring occasionally, until beginning to blister. Add the ginger and garlic, and cook until fragrant, 30 seconds.

4. Pour in the soy sauce and vinegar. Simmer, stirring frequently and breaking up browned bits until the sauce reduces and peas are tender, 2 minutes.

5. Break the tofu into 1-inch pieces and toss in the pan to coat. Remove from the heat and transfer the mixture to the serving bowl. Cool slightly, 2 minutes. Add the maple syrup, mustard, noodles, and cashews, tossing to coat. Top with the green scallion parts and enjoy.

Ingredient Tip: To remove the seeds and membranes from chiles, hold the stem and make an incision down the chile to expose the inside. Using the side of your knife, scrape out the seeds and membranes and discard. Slice off the stem and discard. If you're sensitive to spice or touch your eyes a lot, consider using gloves to prep the chiles!

SHEET PAN GNOCCHI WITH BLISTERED TOMATOES AND BROCCOLI RABE

PREP TIME: 10 MINUTES / COOK TIME: 20 MINUTES

Once you roast gnocchi in the oven and enjoy these golden-brown, crispy-chewy nuggets of joy, it'll be hard to go back to boiling them. Plus, the sheet pan trick is great for quick, all-in-one meals. Roasted garlic (from the same pan) rounds out the "sauce" when whisked with a little balsamic. Want more protein? Toss the pasta with some rotisserie chicken pieces or chunks of fresh mozzarella.

2 to 4 ounces fresh potato gnocchi

½ pint grape or cherry tomatoes

1 medium onion

2 cups chopped broccoli rabe

⅛ teaspoon salt

¼ teaspoon freshly ground black pepper

2 tablespoons plus 1 teaspoon extra-virgin olive oil, divided

1 small head garlic

2 teaspoons balsamic or red wine vinegar

Torn basil leaves, for garnish

Grated Parmesan cheese, for garnish

1. Preheat the oven to 425°F. Line a baking sheet with aluminum foil.

2. Combine the gnocchi, tomatoes, onion, broccoli rabe, salt, and pepper in a large bowl. Drizzle 2 tablespoons of olive oil into the bowl and gently toss to combine. Spread the mixture out evenly on the prepared baking sheet.

3. Slice the top off the garlic head to expose the cloves. Place it on a piece of foil, drizzle with the remaining 1 teaspoon of oil, and wrap up the garlic. Place on the sheet pan.

4. Roast, stirring halfway through and rotating the pan, until the gnocchi are golden, the broccoli is tender, the tomatoes are bursting, and the roasted garlic pouch feels soft when squeezed, 18 to 20 minutes.

5. Remove from the oven and open the garlic pouch to release the steam. When it is cool enough to handle, squeeze the cloves into a serving bowl. Add the vinegar and mash with a fork.

6. Add the gnocchi mixture to the bowl and toss well to combine. Top with the basil and Parmesan and enjoy.

CRISPY CHICKPEA PATTIES WITH GREENS AND CUCUMBER-YOGURT SAUCE

IN A PINCH / PREP TIME: 10 MINUTES / COOK TIME: 10 MINUTES

These patties are similar to falafel, with a little extra crunch from the panko and a kick from the cayenne (if using). Rounded out with a spoonful of tangy cucumber sauce and served on a bed of greens (or stuffed into pita pockets), they make a filling yet light and nutritious lunch or dinner.

3 tablespoons plain Greek yogurt

3 tablespoons chopped cucumber

Zest and 1 teaspoon juice of 1 lemon

⅛ teaspoon freshly ground black pepper

¾ cup canned chickpeas, rinsed, drained

1 tablespoon coarsely chopped fresh parsley

1 large egg

¼ teaspoon ground cumin

¼ teaspoon garlic powder

¼ teaspoon salt

Pinch cayenne pepper (optional)

¼ cup panko bread crumbs

¼ cup avocado or other high-heat oil for frying

2 cups mixed salad greens, frisée, watercress, or spinach

1. In a small bowl, stir together the yogurt, cucumber, lemon zest and juice, and pepper. Cover and refrigerate.

2. In a food processor, combine the chickpeas, parsley, egg, cumin, garlic powder, salt, and cayenne (if using). Pulse a few times until the mixture is blended but still chunky. Do not overprocess. Stir in the panko with a fork and mix well.

3. Form the mixture into three small slider-size patties, about ⅓ cup per patty, and place on a plate.

4. Heat the oil in a medium skillet over medium heat until it just begins to bubble. Add more oil, if needed, to fully coat the skillet. Place the patties in the pan, flattening them a bit with a metal spatula. Cook until they are brown on both sides and cooked through in the center, flipping once, 6 minutes. Reduce the heat if they brown too fast.

5. Remove the patties with a slotted spoon and drain them on a paper towel–lined plate. Serve over the salad greens and topped with the cucumber-yogurt sauce.

Cooking Tip: You can also bake the patties, coated in a thin layer of oil, in a 375°F oven until brown and cooked through, 20 minutes (flipping once, halfway through).

Use It Up: Leftover cucumber can be used for Lemony Hummus Bowl with Cucumber-Tomato-Feta Salad (page 66) or Marinated Vegetable Salad with Fresh Mozzarella (page 31).

LEMONY HUMMUS BOWL WITH CUCUMBER-TOMATO-FETA SALAD

IN A PINCH / PREP TIME: 15 MINUTES, PLUS 2 MINUTES BLENDING TIME

I love this recipe because the tahini and lemon add both creaminess and zing. I find it's nearly impossible to make a very small portion of hummus at a time, unless you have the tiniest of all mini food processors. It just doesn't blend properly, resulting in a chunky, rather than creamy, finish. Instead, I recommend just using the entire can of chickpeas (which makes about 2 cups of hummus) and enjoy it during the week as a snack or light lunch with veggies. It will keep in the refrigerator for up to 2 weeks.

1 (15.5-ounce) can chickpeas, drained, rinsed

¼ cup tahini paste

4 tablespoons extra-virgin olive oil, divided

1 garlic clove

4 lemons, halved, divided

¼ teaspoon salt

¼ teaspoon freshly ground black pepper

1 small shallot, minced

3 tablespoons crumbled feta cheese

1 ripe beefsteak or 2 plum tomatoes, diced, or 1 cup halved cherry tomatoes

1 small cucumber, diced

Fresh mint leaves, cilantro, dill or parsley, for garnish

1. Combine the chickpeas, tahini, 3 tablespoons of olive oil, and garlic in a food processor. Squeeze the juice from 3 lemons into the food processor. Pulse until creamy, 2 minutes. Transfer to a bowl, cover, and refrigerate.

2. Squeeze the juice from the remaining lemon into a medium bowl. Add the remaining 1 tablespoon of olive oil, salt, pepper, and shallot, whisking vigorously. Fold in the feta, tomatoes, and cucumber.

3. Spoon about ½ cup of hummus into a serving bowl. Top with the salad and fresh herbs and enjoy.

Make It Faster: Use store-bought hummus, but only the kind without oil to avoid the refined oils used by some hummus brands.

FARRO WITH CREAMY MUSHROOMS, SPINACH, AND ROSEMARY

IN A PINCH / PREP TIME: 10 MINUTES / COOK TIME: 10 MINUTES

This is a super-fast light lunch or dinner, thanks to the quick-cooking farro and the mushrooms. When cooked properly and caramelized, they make a nice, umami stand-in for meat, with the sour cream and mustard offering a stroganoff-like taste. I'm seeing more and more grocery stores carry "clean label" quick-cooking grains (and pasta) these days, but if you can only find regular farro, cook it according to package directions before making the mushroom mixture—this will take about 15 minutes.

1 tablespoon extra-virgin olive oil

8 ounces cremini mushrooms, wiped clean and cut into ¼-inch pieces

⅛ teaspoon salt

¼ teaspoon freshly ground black pepper

1 garlic clove, minced

1 teaspoon chopped fresh rosemary leaves or ½ teaspoon dried

1 cup loosely packed baby spinach leaves

1 (8.5-ounce) package quick-cooking farro

2 tablespoons Dijon mustard

1 tablespoon sour cream

Grated Parmesan cheese, for garnish

Chopped fresh parsley, for garnish (optional)

1. In a medium skillet, heat the olive oil over medium-high heat. Add the mushrooms in a single layer and cook, without stirring, until they are caramelized on the bottom, 3 minutes. Flip them with a metal spatula and continue to cook, stirring once or twice, until they are caramelized on the other side and the mushrooms release their liquid, 5 minutes. Season with the salt and pepper.

2. Push the mushrooms to the side of the pan. Add the garlic and rosemary and cook until fragrant, 30 seconds. Stir in the spinach and remove from the heat to cool slightly.

3. While the mushroom mixture cools, microwave the farro according to its package directions, 90 seconds. Pour it into a serving bowl. Stir the mustard and sour cream into the mushrooms and place the mixture on the farro. Garnish with the Parmesan and parsley (if using).

Ingredient Tip: To easily remove rosemary leaves from the stem, hold the stem at the top with one hand and run your index finger and thumb down the stem against the direction of the leaves.

Make It Faster: Use precleaned, presliced mushrooms.

RED LENTIL AND TOMATO DAL

PREP TIME: 5 MINUTES / COOK TIME: 20 MINUTES

In culinary terms, "dal" is a term used to describe soups or curries made with dried, split pulses, such as lentils. This quick and easy rendition is fine on its own or goes great with cooked rice, cauliflower rice, quinoa, or naan for soaking up. Diced carrots and peas are added to spike it with a few extra veggies.

1 tablespoon extra-virgin olive or avocado oil

1 small onion, diced

1 small carrot, cut into ¼-inch cubes

1 garlic clove, minced

¼ cup dried red lentils

1 cup water or vegetable stock

½ cup canned diced tomatoes, drained

¼ teaspoon turmeric

¼ teaspoon ground cumin

⅛ teaspoon ground ginger

¼ cup frozen peas

Salt

Freshly ground black pepper

¼ cup chopped fresh cilantro

1 small jalapeño chili, seeded, chopped (optional)

1. Heat the oil in a medium skillet over medium heat. Add the onion and carrot and cook until they're soft and beginning to brown, 5 minutes. Add the garlic and cook until fragrant, 30 seconds.

2. Stir in the lentils, water, tomatoes, turmeric, cumin, and ginger. Cover and bring to a boil. Reduce the heat, keep covered, and simmer until the lentils are tender, 15 minutes. Stir in the peas during the last 2 minutes of simmering time. Turn off the heat and season with salt and pepper.

3. Spoon into a bowl or over cooked rice/grain. Top with cilantro and jalapeño (if using).

RATATOUILLE PASTA WITH TORN BASIL

PREP TIME: 10 MINUTES / COOK TIME: 20 MINUTES

This colorful and antioxidant-rich one-pot wonder was "invented" as a way to use up extra vegetables. Although you may have seen it as a casserole with very thinly sliced vegetables, for this recipe, dicing the veggies into smaller cubes helps them cook faster. If you want more protein, add ½ cup of drained and rinsed cannellini or butter beans to the ratatouille after cooking.

1 small eggplant, cut into ½-inch slices

Salt

2 tablespoons extra-virgin olive oil

¼ cup diced yellow onion

1 small zucchini, cut into ⅛-inch cubes

1 small yellow squash, cut into ⅛-inch cubes

1 garlic clove, minced

1 cup halved cherry tomatoes

1 teaspoon dried oregano

½ teaspoon dried thyme

½ teaspoon freshly ground black pepper

1 cup filtered water

¾ cup dry pasta of choice (farfalle, elbows, etc.)

3 or 4 basil leaves, torn

Grated Parmesan cheese, for garnish (optional)

1. Lay the eggplant slices on a paper towel–lined plate. Season them with salt and let them sit to soften and leach any bitterness while you prepare the remaining ingredients. When you're ready to cook them, cut the eggplant slices into ½-inch cubes.

2. In a medium saucepan or Dutch oven, heat the olive oil over medium heat. Add the onion and cook it until it's soft and translucent, 2 minutes.

3. Add the eggplant, zucchini, and squash, cooking until just softened, 2 minutes. And the garlic and cook until fragrant, 30 seconds. Crush the tomatoes with your hands over the pot.

4. Add the oregano, thyme, pepper, water, and pasta. Cover and bring to a boil. Lower the heat to a simmer and partially remove the lid. Simmer until the vegetables are tender, the pasta is cooked al dente, and the water has evaporated, 10 minutes. Spoon the pasta and sauce onto a plate. Garnish with the basil and Parmesan (if using) and enjoy.

Tip: If you'd rather skip the pasta, you can enjoy the ratatouille over greens or other grains, or even chilled on toast points or salad. Just halve the amount of water. Ratatouille will last in the refrigerator for 3 to 5 days, or freeze it for longer storage.

Make It Faster: Omit the eggplant.

STICKY RICE BOWL WITH PICKLED CARROTS, CUCUMBERS, AND FRIED EGG

PREP TIME: 10 MINUTES / COOK TIME: 20 MINUTES

Sticky rice is most commonly found in sushi, but it's chewy and delicious in this one-pot dish, especially when paired with crunchy carrots and cucumber. White rice works best here, but you could use brown or cauliflower rice; it just might not be as "sticky." The runny yolk from the egg makes a velvety "sauce," but if you'd rather skip the egg, you could brown some extra-firm tofu (or baked tofu) cubes in the same pot with a little toasted sesame oil for extra flavor. Want more veggies? Sauté some baby spinach and mushrooms or mung bean sprouts to add to your bowl.

1 cup shredded carrot

½ cup thinly sliced cucumber

½ teaspoon rice or apple cider vinegar

2¼ teaspoons sesame oil, divided

⅛ teaspoon red pepper flakes

Pinch salt

¼ cup rice

¼ cup water

1 large egg

Freshly ground black pepper

Soy sauce, for garnish

Sesame seeds, for garnish

Thinly sliced scallions, for garnish

Hot sauce or sriracha (optional)

1. In a small bowl, toss the carrot and cucumber with the vinegar, ¼ teaspoon of oil, red pepper flakes, and salt. Set aside.

2. In a small saucepan, combine the rice, water, and 1 teaspoon of oil. Cover and bring it to a boil. Reduce it to a simmer and cook until the liquid has absorbed, 15 minutes. Spoon the rice into a serving bowl and set aside.

3. Wipe out the pot and heat the remaining 1 teaspoon of oil over medium-low heat. Crack the egg into a ramekin and then gently slide the egg into the pot. Cover and cook until it is brown on the bottom and the whites are just set, 3 minutes.

4. Drain the cucumbers and carrots and spoon them over the rice. Top with the egg. Garnish with the soy sauce, sesame seeds, scallions, and sriracha (if using). Enjoy.

Make It Faster: Reheat cooked rice, grain, or cauliflower rice before pairing with the quick-pickled veggies and fried egg. You can also skip the quick-pickling step and just use store-bought pickles, maybe with a few red pepper flakes added.

SWEET POTATO CURRY WITH GREEN BEANS AND TOFU

PREP TIME: 10 MINUTES / COOK TIME: 20 MINUTES

I once had a dish just like this at a restaurant promoting anti-inflammatory foods. It was so comforting and satisfying and I didn't need a nap afterward. Turmeric adds an extra dose of anti-inflammation. A little Greek yogurt rounds out the bowl with some creaminess.

1 cup cubed extra-firm tofu (or baked tofu or tempeh)

⅛ teaspoon salt

⅛ teaspoon freshly ground black pepper

1½ tablespoons coconut oil

2 teaspoons curry powder

1 teaspoon turmeric

¼ cup diced yellow onion

1 garlic clove, minced

2 teaspoons minced ginger

1 heaping tablespoon tomato paste

1 small sweet potato, peeled and cut into 1-inch cubes (1 to 1½ cups)

1 cup halved, trimmed green beans

¾ cup coconut milk

½ cup water

Dollop plain Greek yogurt or sour cream, for garnish (optional)

Lime wedge, for garnish

1. Rinse the tofu, wrap it in a paper towel, and gently squeeze out any excess moisture. Cut it into 1-inch cubes, season with the salt and pepper, and set aside.

2. Heat the oil over medium heat in a deep skillet with a lid. Add the curry powder, turmeric, and onion. Cook, stirring into a paste-like consistency, until it's caramelized and fragrant, 3 minutes. Add the garlic and ginger and cook until fragrant, stirring often, 1 minute. Add the tomato paste and let sit undisturbed to lightly caramelize, 1 minute. Stir to combine. Add the sweet potatoes, beans, coconut milk, and water. Cover and bring to a boil. Reduce to a simmer and cook, uncovered, until the potatoes are softened, 12 to 15 minutes, stirring occasionally.

3. Fold in the tofu. Spoon the curry into a bowl, top with the yogurt (if using), and serve with a lime wedge.

Make It Faster: Use washed, trimmed, bagged green beans and jarred minced ginger and/or garlic.

Use It Up: Use extra tofu for Tofu and Snow Pea Stir-Fry with Soba Noodles (page 63).

STUFFED PORTOBELLO MUSHROOMS WITH WALNUT, SPINACH, AND PARMESAN CRUMBLE

PREP TIME: 10 MINUTES / COOK TIME: 20 MINUTES

Walnuts are an amazing meat replacement in many dishes, including this one, where they add a toothsome, umami richness and a dose of omega-3 fatty acids. I like to use Gorgonzola here because it's creamier than other types of blue cheese, but you can use whatever you have or even substitute another soft, creamy cheese like goat or brie.

2 large portobello mushroom caps

2 teaspoons extra-virgin olive oil

¼ cup walnuts, chopped

¼ cup packed baby spinach leaves, cut into chiffonade (see page 12), plus more for serving if desired

2 tablespoons chopped fresh parsley, plus more for garnish

1 tablespoon unsalted butter, melted

¼ cup crumbled Gorgonzola

2 tablespoons grated Parmesan cheese

Freshly ground black pepper

Vinegar (balsamic, red wine, or apple cider)

1. Heat the oven or toaster oven to 350°F.

2. Remove and coarsely chop any mushroom stems and set aside. Using a small metal spoon, gently scrape out and discard the gills from the caps to reduce moisture. Place the mushroom caps stem-side down on a baking sheet and brush them with the olive oil. Roast until just beginning to soften, 3 minutes.

3. Meanwhile, in a small bowl, toss the chopped mushroom stems, walnuts, spinach, parsley, and butter. Fold in the Gorgonzola.

4. Remove the mushrooms from the oven and turn the caps over. Stuff each evenly with the walnut mixture, pressing down with the back of a spoon to flatten.

5. Return them to the oven and bake until the stuffing is warmed through and the mushrooms release their liquid, 12 to 15 minutes. In the last minute of roasting, top each cap with Parmesan.

6. Place the caps on a plate or bed of spinach. Season with pepper, a splash of vinegar, and parsley, and enjoy.

SPINACH-ARTICHOKE LOADED POTATO

GOOD FOR SCALING / PREP TIME: 10 MINUTES / COOK TIME: 15 MINUTES

People might say I'm obsessed with this dip and its tangy veg, creamy base, and crunchy-cheesy broiled top. Instead of heavy mayo and cream cheese, this recipe calls for blending cooked white beans to lighten up the dish while adding fiber and nutrients. Feel free to substitute a sweet potato for the russet potato, if you prefer.

1 medium russet potato

¼ teaspoon garlic powder

2 tablespoons vegetable stock

2 cups loosely packed baby spinach leaves

1 cup canned or jarred artichoke hearts, drained, chopped

¼ cup shredded mozzarella cheese

⅛ teaspoon red pepper flakes (optional)

¼ cup freshly grated Romano or Parmesan cheese

1. Preheat the oven to 375°F.

2. Pierce the potato with a knife in four places. Wrap it in a damp paper towel and microwave it on High for 5 minutes.

3. Remove the potato and allow it to cool for a minute. Slice off the top of the potato lengthwise. Spoon out most of the flesh and put it into the bowl of a food processor. Place the potato shell on a rimmed baking sheet.

4. Add the garlic powder and stock to the food processor. Pulse until very smooth. Fold in the spinach, artichokes, mozzarella, and red pepper flakes (if using).

5. Spoon the mixture onto the potato. Top it with the cheese and bake until bubbly, 7 to 10 minutes.

Tip: To use this filling as a dip for a crowd, scale up the recipe by using the whole cans/jars of artichoke hearts and serve with crackers and crudités.

SPAGHETTI SQUASH "BOLOGNESE"

PREP TIME: 10 MINUTES / COOK TIME: 20 MINUTES

When I'm looking for a lighter, low-carb sub for pasta and meat sauce, this dual-veggie dish does the trick. Eggplant brings a meatiness to the dish, especially when cooked with some walnuts.

1 small spaghetti squash

1 small eggplant

Salt

2 tablespoons extra-virgin olive oil

1 shallot, thinly sliced

1 or 2 garlic cloves, minced

1 tablespoon tomato paste

⅓ cup chopped walnut halves

¼ teaspoon freshly ground black pepper

¼ teaspoon dried oregano

1 (14.5-ounce) can crushed tomatoes or 2 cups prepared tomato sauce

Grated Parmesan cheese, for garnish

Torn basil leaves, for garnish

⅛ teaspoon red pepper flakes, for garnish (optional)

1. Pierce the spaghetti squash in a few places, put it on a microwave-safe plate, and microwave it on High until it is tender when squeezed on the outside, 10 minutes.

2. Meanwhile, trim the top and bottom off the eggplant and cut it lengthwise into ¼-inch-thick slices. Slice crosswise to dice it and transfer to a paper towel–lined plate. Sprinkle with salt and let it sit while you prepare the other ingredients.

3. Heat the olive oil in a deep skillet over medium-high heat. Roll up the eggplant in the paper towel and squeeze it to release the liquid. Add the eggplant to the skillet until it is brown and beginning to soften, 5 minutes. Add the shallot and garlic and cook until soft and fragrant, 2 minutes. Add the tomato paste and let sit to caramelize, 30 seconds.

4. Stir the mixture and add the walnuts, pepper, oregano, and tomatoes. Cover and bring to a boil. Reduce the heat and simmer, uncovered, until softened and the liquid absorbed, 10 minutes.

5. To serve, slice the squash in half. Spoon out the seeds and discard. Spoon the flesh into a large bowl. Depending on size, use all the squash or freeze half for later use. Top with the eggplant mixture, Parmesan, basil, and red pepper flakes (if using). Enjoy.

Preparation Tip: For an earthier flavor, toast the walnuts in a toaster oven or 350°F oven until brown and fragrant, 3 to 4 minutes. When cool enough to handle, chop them and set aside.

CHARRED CAULIFLOWER STEAK WITH CAULI RICE, RAISINS, AND ALMONDS

PREP TIME: 15 MINUTES / COOK TIME: 18 MINUTES

Loosely inspired by biryani—a rice dish that often includes dried fruits and other add-ins—this recipe features cauliflower two ways for a satisfying balance of textures and to use up the whole vegetable. The almonds and yogurt drizzle round out the dish with a little extra protein and healthy fat.

1 small head cauliflower

2 tablespoons coconut oil or butter, divided, plus more for coating cauliflower

½ teaspoon salt, divided

½ teaspoon freshly ground black pepper, divided

¼ cup diced yellow onion

1 garlic clove, minced

2 teaspoons minced ginger

¼ teaspoon garam masala

⅛ teaspoon ground cinnamon

⅛ teaspoon ground nutmeg

¼ cup raisins

¼ cup water

Chopped cilantro for garnish

Sliced almonds, for garnish

1. Remove the leaves and slice off the cauliflower core. Slice a 2-inch steak from top to bottom. Coat it with oil, season with ¼ teaspoon each of salt and pepper, and set it aside. Finely chop or pulse the remaining cauliflower in a food processor to resemble rice. Set aside.

2. Heat 1 tablespoon of the oil in a deep ceramic or cast-iron skillet (with lid) over medium-high heat. When it's hot, sear the cauliflower until charred on both sides, flipping once, 4 minutes. Set aside.

3. Heat the remaining 1 tablespoon of oil in the skillet over medium heat. Add the onion and cook until golden, 8 minutes. Add the garlic and ginger and cook until fragrant, 1 minute. Add 1½ cups of cauliflower rice, the garam masala, cinnamon, nutmeg, remaining ¼ teaspoon each of salt and pepper, raisins, and water and stir well. Cover and bring to a boil. Reduce the heat to a simmer and cook, uncovered, until all the water has evaporated, stirring occasionally, 5 minutes.

4. Stir in the cilantro and almonds. Spoon onto a plate, top with the cauliflower steak, and enjoy.

Use It Up: Reserve a third of the cauliflower for Sticky Chicken Drumettes and Cauliflower with Homemade Ranch (page 102) or make an extra batch of cauliflower rice by microwaving the rice with a little coconut oil or butter. Cool completely and freeze for later use.

CHAPTER 6

Fish and Seafood

< Garlicky Clam Spaghetti with Cherry Tomatoes, page 81

EASY SHRIMP CEVICHE

PREP TIME: 5 MINUTES, PLUS 25 MINUTES OF REFRIGERATION TIME

Technically, ceviche involves "cooking" raw seafood with citrus juice over a period of several hours. To avoid any risk with potential bacteria and to speed up the prep, this recipe calls for chilled, cooked shrimp, typically available at your grocery store's seafood counter. If you use frozen cooked shrimp, thaw it in a bowl of cold water for 20 minutes.

4 to 6 ounces cooked medium shrimp, peeled and deveined

¼ cup freshly squeezed lemon juice

3 tablespoons freshly squeezed lime juice

1 ripe plum tomato, seeded and chopped

1 small shallot, finely chopped (or quick-pickled red onion from Fish Tacos, page 38)

1 small serrano or jalapeño pepper, seeded, finely chopped

½ cup chopped fresh cilantro leaves and tender stems, plus more if wanted

¼ teaspoon kosher salt

1 small avocado

Tortilla chips, for serving (optional)

1. Chop the shrimp into ½-inch pieces and place them in a large bowl. Add the lemon juice, lime juice, tomato, shallot, serrano, cilantro, and salt, and toss to combine. Cover and refrigerate for at least 25 minutes, and up to 4 hours.

2. Just before serving, dice the avocado, add it to the ceviche, and gently toss to combine. Serve with tortilla chips (if using).

Ingredient Tip: You can also use thawed, cooked frozen shrimp for this recipe.

LEMONY TUNA WITH ORZO, DILL, AND CUCUMBER

IN A PINCH / PREP TIME: 5 MINUTES / COOK TIME: 10 MINUTES

2 ounces dry orzo

1 (6-ounce) can solid white albacore tuna (packed in water), drained

1 small cucumber, diced

1 tablespoon extra-virgin olive oil

Zest from 1 small or ½ medium lemon

½ bunch fresh dill, chopped

Salt

Freshly ground black pepper

1. Cook the orzo according to package directions, about 8 to 10 minutes. Drain and transfer to a serving bowl.

2. Add the tuna, cucumber, olive oil, lemon zest, and dill, tossing to combine. Season with salt and pepper. Cut the lemon into wedges and squeeze over the pasta.

Tip: This dish can be made ahead and chilled overnight for a delicious light lunch or dinner the next day.

PACKET-BAKED FISH AND SQUASH WITH BUTTER BEANS

PREP TIME: 10 MINUTES / COOK TIME: 15 MINUTES

Preparing fish in a parchment paper packet is super easy, and it creates its own delicate herb "sauce" when baked with butter and topped with lemon juice and basil afterward. You could even add a little lemon zest to the packet for an extra pop of brightness.

1 very small zucchini, thinly sliced

1 very small yellow squash, thinly sliced

¼ cup canned butter beans, drained

1 teaspoon extra-virgin olive oil

½ teaspoon dried thyme

Salt

Freshly ground black pepper

1 (4- to 6-ounce) whitefish fillet (e.g., cod, flounder, tilapia)

2 tablespoons cold butter, cubed

2 lemon wedges, for garnish

Torn basil leaves, for garnish

1. Preheat the oven to 425°F.
2. Tear off a 20-inch-long piece of parchment paper and drape it over a glass baking dish so half of it sits in the dish. Fold up the edges to start making the packet.
3. Add the zucchini, squash, beans, olive oil, thyme, and a pinch of salt and pepper, tossing to coat. Place the fish on top and season with more salt and pepper. Dot the butter evenly on top.
4. Fold over the remaining half of the parchment paper, crimping and folding the edges to seal tightly.
5. Bake until the vegetables are tender and the fish is opaque and flaky, 10 to 15 minutes.
6. Remove the packet from the oven and carefully open the pouch to release steam. Transfer the fish to a serving plate, followed by the squash and beans. Squeeze lemon over everything and top with basil. Season with more pepper, if desired, and enjoy.

Use It Up: Leftover zucchini and yellow squash can be used for Ratatouille Pasta with Torn Basil (page 69).

GARLICKY CLAM SPAGHETTI WITH CHERRY TOMATOES

PREP TIME: 10 MINUTES / COOK TIME: 15 MINUTES

My mom regularly made this pantry-friendly meal for us growing up, and it's been a hit with me even as an adult (see the tip below for a gluten-free option). I've also gotten in the habit of adding a small piece of Parmesan cheese rind to the pasta water instead of just salt, for extra umami flavor. To ensure the sauce doesn't break, keep the cubed butter in the refrigerator until just before use.

1 tablespoon extra-virgin olive oil

3 garlic cloves, minced

⅛ teaspoon red pepper flakes

1 (6.5-ounce) can chopped clams

1 cup water

1 cup halved cherry tomatoes

2 ounces dried spaghetti

1 small Parmesan cheese rind (optional)

2 tablespoons cold butter, cubed

Chopped fresh flat-leaf parsley or basil, for garnish

Freshly ground black pepper, for garnish

1 lemon wedge, for garnish

Grated Parmesan cheese, for garnish (optional)

1. Heat the olive oil in a large deep skillet over medium-low heat. Add the garlic and red pepper flakes and cook until fragrant, 3 minutes. Drain the liquid from the clams into the skillet. Add the water, cover, and bring to a simmer. Add the tomatoes and bend and press the spaghetti strands into the liquid to soften (or break the strands in half), stirring until the pasta is mostly submerged. Nestle in the cheese rind, if using.

2. Simmer, uncovered, stirring occasionally, until the pasta is al dente and most of the liquid has evaporated, 8 minutes. Add more water by the tablespoon to cook the pasta fully, if needed.

3. Remove from the heat. Add the clams, tossing to combine. When cooled slightly, stir in the butter, 1 cube at a time.

4. Spoon into a serving bowl and top with the parsley and pepper. Serve with a lemon wedge and grated Parmesan (if using).

Tip: You could easily substitute a gluten-free option such as zucchini noodles (many grocery stores now offer this in the produce aisle) or spaghetti squash (see Spaghetti Squash "Bolognese," page 74) for the spaghetti. Just omit the water and pasta and add the zucchini noodles or cooked spaghetti squash during the last couple minutes of simmering. Note that the sauce won't be as thick because of the missing starch from the pasta.

CHILI-DUSTED SALMON WITH HONEY GLAZED CARROTS

IN A PINCH / PREP TIME: 5 MINUTES / COOK TIME: 15 MINUTES

I learned this trick for "glazing" carrots on the stovetop a while back and have been cooking carrots this way ever since (try coconut oil instead of the butter for a fun flavor change). You can use the same pan to cook both the carrots and the salmon; just make sure it's safe to go in the oven.

1 (6-ounce) salmon fillet (skin removed)

2 teaspoons chili powder

1 tablespoon unsalted butter

1 medium carrot, cut into ½-inch-thick slices (about 1 cup)

1 tablespoon honey

1 cup water

Salt

Freshly ground black pepper

2 teaspoons avocado or extra-virgin olive oil

2 teaspoons chopped fresh cilantro or fresh thyme leaves (optional)

1 scallion, green parts only, for garnish (optional)

1 or 2 lime wedges

1. Pat the salmon dry and rub with the chili powder.

2. Melt the butter in a deep ovenproof skillet with a lid. Add the carrot, honey, and water. Cover and bring to a boil. Remove the cover and cook at a low boil until all the water evaporates, 6 to 8 minutes. Watch the pot closely so the carrots don't burn. Remove the pot from the heat as soon as the water has evaporated, and quickly stir. Transfer it to a serving plate and season the carrots with salt and pepper. Set aside.

3. Wipe out the skillet. Add the oil and heat over medium heat until shimmering. Place the salmon, skin-side down, in the center of the skillet. Cover and cook until just pink in the center, or until it reaches an internal temperature of 120°F, 5 minutes.

4. Place the salmon atop or next to the carrots on the serving plate. Top with the cilantro and scallion (if using), and serve with lime wedges.

CRAB CAKES WITH LEMON CREAM

IN A PINCH / PREP TIME: 10 MINUTES / COOK TIME: 10 MINUTES

I never tire of a good crab cake. It's a little indulgent sometimes, given the price, but lovely for an elegant dinner. Serve these cakes on a bed of butterhead lettuce, baby spinach leaves, or perhaps a little crunchy frisée lightly dressed with lemon juice, extra-virgin olive oil, salt, and pepper.

3 tablespoons sour cream (or plain Greek yogurt)

Zest and 1 teaspoon juice of ½ lemon

1 large egg

6 ounces fresh crabmeat (lump or backfin)

⅓ cup panko bread crumbs

1½ tablespoons Dijon mustard

2 tablespoons chopped fresh parsley, chives, dill or a combination, plus more for garnish

2 tablespoons thinly sliced scallions (green parts only)

½ teaspoon Old Bay seasoning or smoked paprika

¼ teaspoon salt

¼ teaspoon freshly ground black pepper

⅛ teaspoon red pepper flakes (optional)

3 tablespoons avocado or other high-heat oil

Baby spinach leaves, lettuce, or frisée, for serving (optional)

1. Mix the sour cream, lemon zest, and lemon juice in a small bowl. Cover and refrigerate.

2. Beat the egg in a medium bowl. Add the crab, panko, mustard, parsley, scallions, Old Bay seasoning, salt, pepper, and red pepper flakes (if using). Gently mix to combine, without overmixing. Shape the mixture into three balls.

3. Heat the oil in a cast-iron skillet over medium heat. Add the crab cakes, flattening them with a metal spatula. Cook them until they are brown and crispy on both sides, flipping halfway, 8 minutes total.

4. Transfer the crab cakes to a paper towel-lined plate to drain any excess oil. Serve with the baby spinach leaves, lettuce, or frisée (if using), a large dollop of the lemon cream, and extra fresh herbs, if desired.

RED SNAPPER WITH COUSCOUS AND PEAS

PREP TIME: 10 MINUTES / COOK TIME: 15 MINUTES

This one-skillet dish pairs fish, lemon, and dill for a light and bright, balanced meal. If you want to add more veggies, use a frozen medley with peas and diced or sliced carrots, which also cuts down on cooking time.

1 tablespoon avocado or other high-heat oil

1 (6-ounce) red snapper fillet (skin removed)

¼ teaspoon salt

¼ teaspoon freshly ground black pepper

½ cup chicken or vegetable broth

½ cup frozen peas

⅓ cup dry couscous

1 tablespoon unsalted butter

Chopped fresh dill, for garnish

Zest and juice of ½ lemon, for garnish

1. Heat the oil in a medium deep skillet with a lid over medium-high heat. Season the fish with the salt and pepper and place in the skillet, skinless-side up. Cook until beginning to turn opaque, 3 to 4 minutes. Transfer to a plate and set aside.

2. Combine the broth, peas, and couscous in the skillet and bring to a boil over high heat. Turn off the heat and place the fish over the couscous mixture.

3. Cover and let it stand until the liquid is absorbed and the fish is opaque, 5 minutes. Add the butter and cover so the butter melts a little. Fluff the couscous with a fork.

4. Spoon the couscous into a large bowl and top it with the fish. Garnish with dill, lemon zest, and lemon juice and enjoy.

SIZZLING WHITEFISH WITH GREEN OLIVES AND ORANGE

IN A PINCH / PREP TIME: 10 MINUTES / COOK TIME: 10 MINUTES

There's something about the combination of green olives and orange that lends a salty-sweet-perfumy note to whitefish, which, as most of us know, can be a little lacking in flavor on its own. Getting the pan with the butter and oil nice and hot helps "sear" the fish while speeding up the cooking time.

3 tablespoons unsalted butter

1 tablespoon extra-virgin olive oil

⅓ cup sliced, pitted green olives

1 garlic clove, thinly sliced

1 (6-ounce) flaky whitefish fillet (e.g., cod, haddock, or halibut)

¼ teaspoon salt

¼ teaspoon freshly ground black pepper

Zest and juice of 1 small navel orange

Baby spinach leaves (or other lettuce greens) for serving (optional)

1. Preheat the oven to 350°F.

2. Melt the butter and olive oil in an oven-safe skillet over medium heat until sizzling, 1 to 2 minutes. Stir in the olives and garlic, cooking until fragrant, 1 minute.

3. Nestle the fish in the skillet. Season with salt and pepper. Spoon the butter mixture over the fish to baste it and transfer the fish to the oven.

4. Bake the fish until it is opaque and flaky, basting halfway through with the butter, 8 minutes.

5. Remove the fish from the oven. Stir in the orange zest and juice, basting the fish with the sauce.

6. Place the fish on a bed of baby spinach (if using) and spoon sauce over all. Enjoy.

Use It Up: Use the other orange half for Crunchy Endive, Carrot, and Orange Salad with Creamy Citrus Vinaigrette (page 30).

ONE-POT SHRIMP AND GRITS WITH TOMATOES, PEPPERS, AND PEAS

PREP TIME: 10 MINUTES / COOK TIME: 20 MINUTES

New Orleans meets Lowcountry with this Creole-seasoned shrimp and grits dish made quicker with quick-cooking grits. Feel free to double the spice blend and store it in an airtight container for use in fish and poultry dishes—it's also delicious sprinkled on roasted cauliflower and poached eggs.

FOR THE SPICE BLEND

1 teaspoon dried thyme

1 teaspoon dried oregano

½ teaspoon sweet paprika

½ teaspoon smoked paprika

½ to 1 teaspoon cayenne pepper

¼ teaspoon garlic powder

¼ teaspoon onion powder

¼ teaspoon salt

¼ teaspoon freshly ground black pepper

FOR THE SHRIMP AND GRITS

½ cup chicken or vegetable stock

¼ cup quick-cooking grits

2 tablespoons unsalted butter

½ to 1 cup sharp cheddar cheese, Gruyère, or your choice

Salt

Freshly ground black pepper

2 teaspoons extra-virgin olive oil

1 garlic clove, minced

1 scallion, green and white parts separated

¼ cup diced red or green bell pepper

3 to 4 ounces peeled and deveined medium shrimp (frozen or fresh)

½ cup canned diced tomatoes or fire-roasted diced tomatoes and juices

Chopped fresh parsley, for garnish (optional)

TO MAKE THE SPICE BLEND

1. Combine the thyme, oregano, paprikas, cayenne, garlic powder, onion powder, salt, and pepper in a small bowl and stir. Set aside.

TO MAKE THE SHRIMP AND GRITS

2. Pour the stock into a deep skillet. Cover and bring to a boil. Reduce the heat to a simmer and add the grits, stirring vigorously to prevent lumps, 1 minute. Simmer, uncovered, stirring occasionally, until the stock is fully absorbed and the grits are thickened, 10 minutes.

3. Remove from the heat. Stir in the butter and cheese, season with salt and pepper, and pour into a serving bowl. Cover loosely with aluminum foil and set aside.

4. Wipe out the skillet and heat the olive oil over medium heat. Add the garlic, scallion white parts, and bell pepper, and cook until fragrant and starting to soften, 2 minutes.

5. Add the shrimp, tomatoes, and spice blend, stirring to coat. Cover and simmer on low until the shrimp are cooked through, 3 to 5 minutes (depending on if you're using raw or frozen shrimp).

6. Remove the lid and simmer until the liquid reduces further, 2 minutes.

7. Pour the mixture over the grits, and top with the green scallion parts and parsley (if using). Enjoy warm.

Make It Faster: Purchase prepared Creole seasoning.

Use It Up: Extra grits would go well with Salsa-Baked Eggs (page 22).

SEARED TUNA STEAK WITH SHAVED FENNEL AND CARROT SLAW

PREP TIME: 15 MINUTES / COOK TIME: 10 MINUTES

This take on a seared tuna salad features the delicate flavor of fennel. I'm addicted to it, but I admit that working with fennel takes a little finesse. Once you've mastered handling the perfumy, anise-flavored vegetable, it can stand in for celery as an elegant upgrade.

1 (6-ounce) tuna steak (about 1½-inches thick)

Salt

Freshly ground black pepper

2 tablespoons extra-virgin olive oil

Juice from ½ lemon

1 garlic clove, minced

1 teaspoon Dijon mustard

1 large carrot

1 fennel bulb

2 teaspoons avocado or other high-heat oil

Pistachios, for garnish (optional)

1. Season the tuna liberally with salt and pepper and set aside.
2. In a large bowl, whisk the olive oil, lemon juice, garlic, mustard, salt, and pepper vigorously until it's creamy.
3. Peel the carrot into thin shavings over the dressing.
4. Chop off the fennel stalks and fronds, reserving the stalks for another use. Coarsely chop the fronds and set aside. Slice the bulb in half, removing any discolored outer pieces. Using the vegetable peeler, peel one fennel half, working inward toward the core, so the pieces fall into the bowl. Discard the core. Save the remaining fennel half for other uses. Toss the slaw with the dressing. Refrigerate until ready to serve.
5. Heat the avocado oil in a medium skillet. Sear the tuna until crispy on the outside and pink on the inside, flipping halfway, 6 minutes total. Transfer to a chopping board to rest for 5 minutes.
6. To serve, transfer the slaw to a plate or large bowl. Slice the tuna into thin strips and place atop the slaw. Garnish with pistachios (if using) and reserved fennel fronds.

Use It Up: Leftover fennel bulb can be used for Seafood Stew with Fennel and Rouille Toast (page 52). Slice the stalks into thin pieces and use in place of celery for Chicken and Rice Noodle Soup (page 55).

HERB-BAKED ARCTIC CHAR WITH FINGERLING POTATOES

PREP TIME: 10 MINUTES / COOK TIME: 20 MINUTES

Arctic char has a rich, flavorful taste, somewhere between trout and salmon; that said, feel free to substitute it for those other types of fish, if you prefer, based on what's available and the price. Seasoning the fish in a blend of oil and herbs and then baking it at a lower temperature prevents it from drying out and creates a flavorful sauce for this one-dish dinner. Ask your fishmonger to remove the skin and any bones from the fish.

¾ cup extra-virgin olive oil

1 cup chopped fresh herbs (e.g., parsley, cilantro, chives, dill, or a combination)

Zest from 1 lemon

1 (6- to 8-ounce) arctic char fillet, skin removed

¼ teaspoon salt

¼ teaspoon freshly ground black pepper

1 cup very thinly sliced fingerling potatoes

1. Preheat the oven to 325°F.

2. In a small bowl, mix together the olive oil, herbs, and lemon zest.

3. Place the fish in the center of a small glass baking dish and season it with the salt and pepper. Pour almost all of the herb mixture over the fish, spreading evenly with a rubber spatula.

4. Spread the potatoes in the pan in a single layer around and tucked underneath the fish. Top the potatoes with the remaining herb mixture, coating them evenly.

5. Bake until the potatoes are tender and the fish is opaque on the top and slightly pink in the center, or its internal temperature reaches 120°F, 15 to 20 minutes.

6. Transfer potatoes and fish to a plate. Cut the lemon into 4 wedges, squeeze over all, and enjoy.

Preparation Tip: If you have time, marinate the fish for 3 hours, up to overnight, for extra tenderness and flavor. Just be sure to take it out of the refrigerator 30 minutes before baking it.

SEAFOOD PANCAKE WITH TANGY DIPPING SAUCE

PREP TIME: 15 MINUTES / COOK TIME: 10 MINUTES

I drew inspiration from *haemul pajeon*, a Korean-style pancake studded with seafood and scallions, and *okonomiyaki*, a cabbage-based Japanese pancake often made with shrimp, for this umami-bomb of a meal. Using smoked oysters adds a deeper flavor and is easier for prep, especially when paired with precooked shrimp.

1 large egg

¼ cup all-purpose flour

½ teaspoon baking powder

⅛ teaspoon salt

¼ cup chopped Napa cabbage

1 scallion, thinly sliced

1 teaspoon minced ginger

½ (3.7-ounce) can smoked oysters, drained, patted dry, chopped

1 ounce cooked, peeled, deveined shrimp (or frozen, thawed), cut into ½-inch pieces

1 tablespoon maple syrup

1 tablespoon soy sauce

1 tablespoon rice or apple cider vinegar

1 teaspoon Dijon mustard

¼ teaspoon sesame seeds

¼ teaspoon sesame oil

2 tablespoons avocado or other high-heat oil

1. In a large mixing bowl, beat the egg. Add the flour, baking powder, and salt, mixing well. Mix in the cabbage, scallion, and ginger. Fold in the oysters and shrimp and set aside.

2. In a small bowl, whisk together the maple syrup, soy sauce, vinegar, mustard, sesame seeds, and sesame oil. Set aside.

3. Heat the avocado oil in a medium skillet over medium heat, brushing to coat with a clean spatula.

4. Pour the batter into the pan, spreading it out with the spatula to create a pancake 6 to 7 inches in diameter. Cover the skillet with a large lid and cook until the pancake is brown, flipping halfway through, 7 to 8 minutes total. Watch it carefully and reduce the heat to prevent burning.

5. Transfer the pancake to a plate. Serve with the dipping sauce on the side.

Make It Faster: Tonkatsu sauce from the Chicken Tenders with Tonkatsu and Coleslaw recipe (page 105) would work well as a dipping sauce here if you already have that made or want to make an extra batch for this and the chicken tender recipe.

Use It Up: Leftover coleslaw mix, also from Chicken Tenders with Tonkatsu and Coleslaw (page 105), can be used here. Try extra smoked oysters in Lemony Tuna with Orzo, Dill, and Cucumber (page 79) for an extra pop of savory.

HALIBUT AND GREEN BEANS WITH CHERMOULA

PREP TIME: 5 MINUTES / COOK TIME: 25 MINUTES

Chermoula is a flavorful herb- and spice-based condiment typically served with fish and seafood. Though many variations exist, here we're combining cilantro and parsley with cumin, coriander, and a touch of heat.

1½ cups trimmed, halved green beans

2 teaspoons extra-virgin olive oil, divided, plus 2 to 3 tablespoons

¼ teaspoon salt, divided

¼ teaspoon freshly ground pepper, divided

¼ cup finely chopped fresh cilantro leaves

¼ cup finely chopped parsley leaves

1 garlic clove, minced

2 tablespoons freshly squeezed lemon juice

½ teaspoon ground cumin

¼ teaspoon ground coriander

⅛ teaspoon red pepper flakes

1 (6-ounce) halibut fillet

1. Preheat the oven to 450°F.
2. Put the beans on a large piece of aluminum foil. Toss with 1 teaspoon of oil and ⅛ teaspoon each of salt and pepper. Fold the foil over, sealing tightly to form a packet. Place the packet in a glass baking dish and bake until beginning to soften, 10 to 12 minutes.
3. Meanwhile, combine the cilantro, parsley, 2 to 3 tablespoons of olive oil, garlic, lemon juice, cumin, coriander, and red pepper flakes in a small bowl and whisk with a fork. Set aside.
4. Remove the pan from the oven. Push the package to one side and add the fish. Rub the fish with the remaining teaspoon of oil and season with the remaining salt and pepper. Bake until opaque and flaky, 12 minutes more.
5. To serve, transfer the fish to a plate and top with the chermoula. Serve with the green beans, and, if desired, cooked couscous or quinoa to round out the meal.

Make It Faster: You can make the chermoula in a food processor, but it works better if you double the recipe to do so and then save the rest. Place the cilantro, parsley, and garlic in the bowl of a food processor and pulse until finely chopped. Add the lemon juice, cumin, coriander, salt, and red pepper flakes. With the motor running, add the olive oil and process until well-combined but still chunky. Add more oil or cold filtered water, 1 teaspoon at a time, to thin, if needed.

BLACK COD EN BRODO WITH GINGERY BOK CHOY AND MUSHROOMS

IN A PINCH / PREP TIME: 10 MINUTES / COOK TIME: 10 MINUTES

I love the elegance of this dish, thanks to the gingery and savory light "sauce" (*en brodo* means "in broth") that requires a spoon for slurping, but it's not thin enough to make it a soup, per se. Black cod (also marketed as sablefish or butterfish) is a super delicate and flavorful fish that's meaty enough to handle a little poaching, and it's loaded with healthy omega-3 fatty acids.

1 small head baby bok choy, halved and rinsed

2 teaspoons sesame oil

1 scallion, chopped, white and green parts separated

1 cup thinly sliced cremini (or shiitake, or mixed) mushrooms

1 garlic clove, thinly sliced

1 tablespoon minced ginger

¼ cup vegetable or chicken stock or water

2 tablespoons soy sauce

¼ teaspoon freshly ground black pepper (or ⅛ teaspoon freshly ground Sichuan peppercorns)

1 (6-ounce) piece black cod

1 lime wedge

Sesame seeds, for garnish (optional)

1. Thinly slice each half of the white bok choy bulb, discarding the ends, and set aside. Tear the green leaves into medium pieces and set aside.

2. Heat the oil over medium heat in a deep skillet that also has a lid. Add the scallion white parts, white bok choy parts, and mushrooms. Cook until the vegetables begin to soften, 4 minutes. Add the garlic and ginger and cook until fragrant, 1 minute. Add the stock and soy sauce. Cover the skillet and bring to a slow simmer. Cook until the vegetables begin to soften, 2 minutes.

3. Remove the lid and nestle in the fish. Season with the pepper, cover, and continue to simmer until the fish is opaque, 5 minutes. Turn off the heat and add the bok choy leaves and scallion green parts. Stir until just wilted.

4. To serve, spoon the fish and vegetables into a large bowl using a slotted spoon. Pour in the broth. Squeeze the lime over all and garnish with sesame seeds (if using). Enjoy warm.

Preparation Tip: For a heartier meal, serve with cooked udon, rice, or soba noodles, or sticky rice from Sticky Rice Bowl with Pickled Carrots, Cucumbers, and Fried Egg (page 70).

CHAPTER 7

Poultry and Meat

< Sheet Pan Chicken Fajitas,
  page 96

SHEET PAN CHICKEN FAJITAS

GOOD FOR SCALING / PREP TIME: 10 MINUTES / COOK TIME: 20 MINUTES

This is my go-to weeknight dinner when I don't have a lot of time to fuss over anything but want a balanced, satisfying meal. You can serve the fajitas with warmed flour or corn tortillas, or make a bowl and serve it over rice or lettuce with optional garnishes.

1 teaspoon chili powder

1 teaspoon ground cumin

½ teaspoon dried oregano

¼ teaspoon salt

¼ teaspoon freshly ground black pepper

1 (6-ounce) boneless skinless chicken breast, cut into thin strips (or 6 ounces chicken tenders)

½ red bell pepper, cut into strips

½ yellow or orange bell pepper, cut into strips

½ red onion, thinly sliced

1 garlic clove, minced

1 tablespoon extra-virgin olive oil

1 lime wedge

Quick guacamole (see Tip) (optional)

Sour cream (or Cilantro Cream, see page 62) (optional)

Prepared salsa (optional)

1. Preheat the oven to 425°F.

2. In a small bowl, combine the chili powder, cumin, oregano, salt, and pepper.

3. Place the chicken, bell pepper, onion, and garlic on a rimmed baking sheet. Drizzle with the olive oil and add the spice blend, tossing to combine. Spread out in an even layer.

4. Bake until the chicken is completely cooked through and the vegetables are crisp-tender, 18 to 20 minutes. Squeeze lime juice over all and serve with guacamole, sour cream, and salsa, if using.

Preparation Tip: You can make a super quick guacamole by using a fork to mash ripe avocado in a small bowl with a little freshly squeezed lime juice, a pinch of salt, and if desired, some chopped cilantro and/or prepared salsa.

SAUSAGE, PEPPERS, AND ONIONS WITH POLENTA

PREP TIME: 5 MINUTES / COOK TIME: 20 MINUTES

This riff on the classic Italian-American dish (or hoagie sandwich) of sausage, peppers, and onions features a bed of toasted polenta instead of a bun for a more "dinner-y" dish that's pretty quick and easy to make. Just look for the best butcher-style Italian sausage you can find, or reach for precooked chicken Italian sausage and reduce the simmering time for the meat.

1 tablespoon, plus 1 teaspoon extra-virgin olive oil, divided

2 or 3 slices (1-inch thick) polenta (from an 18-ounce package)

1 link (about 4 ounces) mild or hot Italian sausage

½ yellow onion, cut into ¼-inch-thick pieces

1 red, yellow, or orange bell pepper, stemmed, seeded, cut into ¼-inch-thick pieces

1 garlic clove, thinly sliced

1 tablespoon balsamic vinegar

1½ cups prepared marinara or canned tomato sauce

Grated Parmesan cheese, for garnish

Torn basil leaves, for garnish

1. Heat 1 tablespoon of olive oil in a skillet over medium heat. Add the polenta and cook until heated through, 2 minutes per side. Transfer the polenta to a serving plate and cover it with aluminum foil to keep warm.

2. In the same skillet, cook the sausage until it is brown on all sides, 5 minutes. Transfer it to the plate with the polenta.

3. Add the remaining 1 teaspoon of oil and the onion and cook until it is soft and translucent, 2 minutes. Add the bell pepper and continue to cook until the onion is caramelized, 3 more minutes. Add the garlic and cook until fragrant, 30 seconds.

4. Add the vinegar, scraping up the browned bits. When the liquid evaporates, pour in the marinara. Nestle the sausage in the sauce, cover, and cook until its internal temperature reaches 160°F and the peppers are soft, 8 to 10 minutes. Transfer the sausage to the plate with the polenta and spoon sauce over all. Top with Parmesan cheese and basil and enjoy.

PORK NOODLES WITH CHILI OIL

IN A PINCH / PREP TIME: 10 MINUTES / COOK TIME: 10 MINUTES

Inspired by the popular Sichuan street food, dan dan noodles, this flavorful dish makes a great stand-in for takeout on nights you want a little comfort food. Not a huge fan of heat? Reduce the amount of red pepper flakes and skip the Sichuan peppercorns. You can also substitute just about any other noodle for the wheat noodles. Try rice, gluten-free, spaghetti, zucchini spirals, or even tofu-based noodles.

2 ounces uncooked Chinese-style egg noodles

3 tablespoons sesame oil

1 tablespoon red pepper flakes

¼ teaspoon sesame seeds

⅛ teaspoon cracked Sichuan peppercorns (optional)

3 ounces ground pork

¼ teaspoon salt

¼ teaspoon freshly ground black pepper

2 teaspoons avocado oil

1 cup mixed mushrooms (e.g., cremini, shiitake), chopped

1 scallion, thinly sliced (white and green parts separated)

2 garlic cloves, thinly sliced

2 tablespoons soy sauce

1 cup packed baby spinach leaves

Sesame seeds, for garnish

Lime wedges, for garnish

1. Bring water to a boil in a small saucepan. Add the noodles and cook until softened, 5 minutes, or according to package directions. Drain all but 2 tablespoons of cooking water. Set the noodles aside.

2. Meanwhile, in a small microwave-safe bowl, combine the sesame oil, red pepper flakes, sesame seeds, and Sichuan peppercorns (if using). Microwave on 60 percent power until very fragrant and dark red in color, stirring once or twice, 3 minutes. Set aside to cool.

3. Season the pork with the salt and pepper. Heat the avocado oil in a medium skillet over medium heat. Add the pork and mushrooms and cook, stirring to break it up, until the pork is brown and the mushrooms have released their liquid, 5 minutes.

4. Push the mixture aside and add the white scallion parts and garlic. Cook until fragrant, 1 minute.

5. Turn off the heat. Stir in the soy sauce, spinach, and noodles, tossing until the spinach wilts. Toss with the oil mixture and transfer to a bowl. Garnish with sesame seeds, green scallion parts, and lime wedges and enjoy.

Preparation Tip: You can make a bigger batch of chili oil and store it in a jar in the refrigerator for up to 3 weeks. Remove it from the refrigerator 30 minutes before use to bring it to room temperature. Enjoy the oil with eggs and tofu, in fish dishes, or in other noodle and pasta dishes.

ROAST PORK TENDERLOIN, BRUSSELS SPROUTS, AND APPLES WITH MAPLE-MUSTARD SAUCE

PREP TIME: 10 MINUTES / COOK TIME: 20 MINUTES

Pork, especially when rubbed with delicious spices, pairs well with both Brussels sprouts and apples, so I've combined them here, along with a sweet and savory maple-mustard sauce for dipping or drizzling. Preheating the skillet in the oven helps sear the pork without the extra steps and time on the stovetop.

¼ teaspoon garlic powder

¼ teaspoon onion powder

¼ teaspoon paprika

¼ teaspoon kosher salt

⅛ teaspoon coarsely ground black pepper

1 (6-ounce) piece pork tenderloin

1 tablespoon plus 2 teaspoons avocado or extra-virgin olive oil, divided

2 cups trimmed, halved Brussels sprouts

½ small apple, cored, diced

2 tablespoons maple syrup

2 tablespoons stone-ground mustard

1. Place a cast-iron skillet in the oven and preheat to 450°F.

2. Combine the garlic powder, onion powder, paprika, salt, and pepper in a small bowl. Pat the pork dry and rub with the spices to cover completely.

3. Using oven mitts, remove the skillet from the oven and pour in 1 tablespoon of oil. Give the skillet a swirl so the olive oil coats the entire bottom.

4. Place the pork in the center of the skillet. In a bowl, toss the sprouts and apple with the remaining 2 teaspoons of oil and spread around the pork. Return the skillet to the oven and bake until the pork is cooked through and the sprouts and apples are tender, flipping the pork halfway through and stirring the other ingredients, 20 minutes total.

5. Meanwhile, in a small bowl, stir together the maple syrup and mustard. Set aside.

6. Let the pork rest for at least 5 minutes to retain juiciness, or until its internal temperature reaches 145°F. Slice into 2-inch-thick pieces. Plate the pork with the sprouts, apples, and maple-mustard sauce drizzled over all or in a ramekin for dipping.

Use It Up: Leftover apple slices can be used for Baked Cinnamon-Apple Crisp (page 118). Toss slices with a little lemon juice to prevent browning if storing in the refrigerator for later use.

PAPRIKA CHICKEN THIGHS WITH ROMESCO SAUCE AND TURMERIC RICE

PREP TIME: 10 MINUTES / COOK TIME: 20 MINUTES

I am seriously addicted to this Catalonian-style sauce, and it's made with ingredients you might already have in your pantry. For extra flavor, use a combination of almonds and unsalted, roasted hazelnuts if you can find them, or toasted walnuts—basically any roasted nut you might have on hand works, although hazelnuts are most traditional.

2 or 3 bone-in chicken thighs

2½ teaspoons paprika, divided

¼ teaspoon salt

½ teaspoon freshly ground black pepper, divided

1 (7- to 8-ounce) jar roasted red peppers, drained, rinsed (save and clean the jar)

⅓ cup unsalted raw or blanched almonds

1 garlic clove, smashed

2 tablespoons red wine vinegar

¼ cup extra-virgin olive oil

½ teaspoon turmeric

1 cup cooked rice or cauliflower rice, warmed with a little butter, coconut oil, or olive oil

1 to 2 tablespoons chopped fresh parsley, for garnish (optional)

1. Preheat the oven to 475°F.

2. Place the chicken thighs in a glass or rimmed baking sheet. Combine 2 teaspoons of the paprika, the salt, and ¼ teaspoon of pepper in a small bowl, then rub the mixture all over the chicken.

3. Bake the chicken until it's fully cooked through or until the internal temperature reads 165°F, 20 minutes.

4. Meanwhile, combine the red peppers, almonds, garlic, vinegar, remaining ½ teaspoon of paprika, and remaining ¼ teaspoon of pepper in a blender or food processor. Pulse a few times until the mixture is chunky. Add the olive oil and process until smooth. Pour into the reserved clean jar and set aside.

5. Sprinkle the turmeric over the warm rice and stir to color the rice completely. Spoon the rice onto a plate and top with the chicken. Drizzle a couple tablespoons of sauce over all, garnish with parsley (if using), and enjoy.

Make It Faster: Use 90-second or quick-cooking rice or cook the rice in a small saucepan according to package directions while the chicken bakes.

Use It Up: Double the romesco recipe to use the whole jar of peppers and enjoy on eggs, with vegetable and fish dishes, or tossed with pasta. It will last in the refrigerator for a week, or store it in a resealable plastic bag and flatten to freeze for longer storage.

STEAKHOUSE DINNER WITH ASPARAGUS, SMASHED POTATOES, AND HERB BUTTER

PREP TIME: 10 MINUTES / COOK TIME: 20 MINUTES

This luxurious meal is actually pretty easy to put together, especially when relying on the microwave for the potatoes and cast iron to create that caramelized crust. Note: You might want to make sure your hood fan is on high and/or crack a window. The stovetop sear really is worth it, though.

1 (6- to 8-ounce) boneless rib eye or filet steak

Salt

Freshly ground black pepper

5 ounces baby fingerling potatoes

2 to 3 tablespoons unsalted butter, at room temperature

1 teaspoon chopped fresh parsley

½ bunch medium-thick asparagus (6 or 7 stalks), ends removed

1 to 2 teaspoons extra-virgin olive oil

Grated Parmesan cheese (optional)

1 tablespoon avocado or other high-heat oil

Lemon wedge, for garnish

1. Preheat the oven or toaster oven to 425°F.
2. Pat the steak dry and season each side liberally with salt and pepper. Set aside.
3. Place the potatoes in a microwave-safe bowl filled with about an inch of water. Microwave on high until softened, 5 to 7 minutes.
4. Meanwhile, in a small bowl, mix together the butter and parsley. Refrigerate until ready to serve.
5. Place the asparagus on one side of a rimmed baking sheet. Drain and place the potatoes on the other side. Using a fork, smash each potato so it's thin. Coat the vegetables lightly with the olive oil and, if using, top evenly with the cheese. Roast until the asparagus is tender and the potatoes crisp, 8 minutes.
6. While the vegetables roast, heat the avocado oil in a cast-iron skillet over high heat. When the oil is very hot and smoking, sear the steak until it's brown, turning once, 3 to 5 minutes per side. Remove the steak from the skillet when the internal temperature reaches 125°F (the temperature will continue to rise 10 degrees for medium-rare) and place it on a serving plate. Spoon the chilled herb butter on top of the steak.
7. Add the potatoes and asparagus to the plate. Squeeze lemon juice over the asparagus and enjoy.

STICKY CHICKEN DRUMETTES AND CAULIFLOWER WITH HOMEMADE RANCH

GOOD FOR SCALING / PREP TIME: 10 MINUTES / COOK TIME: 20 MINUTES

When you're craving wings for game day but want to make your own baked version, this is a great go-to recipe that can easily be scaled up to feed a crowd. The combination of soy and honey makes these nuggets addictively sweet and savory.

FOR THE HOMEMADE RANCH

⅓ cup Greek yogurt

Juice from ½ small lemon

1 teaspoon garlic powder

½ teaspoon onion powder

1 teaspoon chopped
fresh chives

1 teaspoon chopped fresh,
flat-leaf parsley

½ teaspoon chopped fresh dill

Pinch salt

Pinch freshly ground
black pepper

FOR THE SAUCE

3 tablespoons unsalted butter

3 tablespoons honey

3 tablespoons soy sauce

1 tablespoon rice vinegar

2 garlic cloves, minced

1 teaspoon minced ginger (or
½ teaspoon ground)

FOR THE CHICKEN

3 tablespoons baking powder

½ teaspoon smoked paprika

½ teaspoon garlic powder

½ teaspoon onion powder

½ teaspoon salt

¼ teaspoon freshly ground
black pepper

2 chicken drumettes

2 cups cauliflower florets

Sesame seeds (optional)

Thinly sliced scallions
(optional)

1. Preheat the oven to 425°F.

TO MAKE THE HOMEMADE RANCH

2. In a small bowl, whisk together the yogurt, lemon juice, garlic powder, onion powder, chives, parsley, dill, salt, and pepper and refrigerate until ready to serve.

TO MAKE THE SAUCE

3. Melt the butter in a small saucepan over medium-low heat. Add the honey, soy sauce, vinegar, garlic, and ginger and stir until it is lightly simmering and thickened, 4 minutes. Remove from the heat and set the saucepan on a kitchen towel or hot plate on the counter where you have room to dip the chicken.

TO MAKE THE CHICKEN

4. While the sauce cools, mix together the baking powder, paprika, garlic powder, onion powder, salt, and pepper in a shallow bowl.

5. Working one by one, dip the chicken and cauliflower in the spice mixture, coating completely. Shake off any excess, then dredge the chicken and cauliflower in the mixture in the saucepan. Place them on a rimmed baking sheet, spaced apart.

6. Bake until they are caramelized and cooked through, flipping and tossing halfway through, 20 minutes.

7. Remove the chicken and cauliflower from the oven and transfer to a plate. Top with sesame seeds and scallions (if using), and serve with the ranch for dipping.

Ingredient Tip: Want a vegetarian option? Skip the chicken and use half a cauliflower head, broken into florets.

BROILED STEAK WITH SPINACH CHIMICHURRI AND "BAKED" SWEET POTATO

GOOD FOR SCALING / PREP TIME: 10 MINUTES / COOK TIME: 15 MINUTES

I enjoy chimichurri with just about everything, but this Argentine herb-forward condiment traditionally pairs with steak. You can always make a little extra chimichurri to keep in your refrigerator for a couple weeks and keep adding chopped parsley and/or cilantro to it as the herbs start to turn. Just let the jar sit out for about 30 minutes before use to soften the oil (it congeals a bit in the refrigerator, and that's okay).

FOR THE STEAK AND POTATO

6 ounces skirt, sirloin, or flat-iron steak

Salt

Freshly ground black pepper

1 small or medium sweet potato

FOR THE CHIMICHURRI

½ cup packed baby spinach leaves, chopped

¼ cup chopped fresh flat-leaf parsley

3 tablespoons extra-virgin olive oil

1 tablespoon red wine vinegar or apple cider vinegar

1 garlic clove, minced

⅛ teaspoon red pepper flakes

TO MAKE THE STEAK AND POTATO

1. Place a cast-iron skillet or pan in the broiler on a rack positioned just underneath the heat source. Preheat it on high.

2. Season the steak liberally with salt and pepper. Set aside.

3. Pierce the sweet potato with a knife a few times. Microwave on high until it is soft in the inside and caramelizing around the edges, 6 to 8 minutes.

TO MAKE THE CHIMICHURRI

4. Meanwhile, combine the spinach, parsley, olive oil, vinegar, garlic, red pepper flakes, and a pinch each of salt and pepper in a small bowl and stir well. Set aside.

5. Carefully remove the hot skillet from the broiler and add the steak. Return the skillet to the broiler and cook until the steak is seared on both sides and the internal temperature reads 125°F for medium-rare or 135°F for medium (temperature will rise 10 more degrees while resting), flipping once, 10 minutes total. Transfer the steak to a serving plate and allow it to rest for 5 minutes.

6. Place the potato on a plate. Cut it open and top the potato and steak with dollops of chimichurri. Enjoy.

CHICKEN TENDERS WITH TONKATSU AND COLESLAW

PREP TIME: 10 MINUTES / COOK TIME: 15 MINUTES

Drawing inspiration from the Japanese street food tonkatsu, this recipe swaps the breaded pork cutlet for chicken tenders. The dipping sauce in this recipe and the creamy cabbage slaw hint at the other key ingredients of the popular sandwich: tonkatsu sauce, Japanese mayo, and Napa cabbage.

1 cup coleslaw mix

¼ cup plain Greek yogurt

1 tablespoon apple cider vinegar

3 tablespoons baking powder

½ teaspoon garlic powder

½ teaspoon onion powder

½ teaspoon salt

¼ teaspoon freshly ground black pepper

1 large egg, beaten

¼ cup panko bread crumbs

1 (6-ounce) boneless, skinless chicken breast, cut into 2-inch pieces, or 6 ounces uncooked chicken tender pieces

1 tablespoon ketchup or tomato paste

2½ teaspoons Worcestershire sauce

1½ teaspoons soy sauce

1 tablespoon maple syrup

1. Preheat the oven to 425°F.

2. Combine the coleslaw mix, yogurt, and vinegar in a medium bowl, cover, and refrigerate until ready to serve.

3. In a small shallow bowl, mix together the baking powder, garlic powder, onion powder, salt, and pepper. Put the egg in a second small, shallow bowl, and the panko in a third.

4. Working one piece at a time, dredge the chicken first in the spices, shaking off excess, then in the egg. Allow the excess to drip off, then dredge the chicken in panko and place it on a rimmed baking sheet.

5. Bake until the chicken is crispy and cooked through, when the internal temperature reaches 165°F, 15 minutes.

6. Meanwhile mix together the ketchup, Worcestershire sauce, soy sauce, and maple syrup in a small bowl.

7. Place the chicken tenders on a plate and serve them with the coleslaw and tonkatsu sauce. Enjoy.

Make It Faster: Purchase prepared tonkatsu sauce from an Asian grocery store or the international section of a higher-end grocery store, but note that these products often have added sugars and sometimes preservatives.

Use It Up: Double the recipe to marinate the coleslaw overnight for a salad the next day, or stuff it into Fish Tacos with Quick-Pickled Red Onions and Smoky Chili Cream (page 38).

PAN-FRIED PORK CHOP WITH CREAMY BEANS AND GREENS

PREP TIME: 10 MINUTES / COOK TIME: 15 MINUTES

This is such a hearty yet balanced dish; cannellini beans become extra creamy when simmered and stirred with a butter-based pan sauce, and they pair nicely with the pork and delicate greens. Splashing vinegar over the dish just before serving adds brightness without causing the Swiss chard to brown.

1 (6-ounce) bone-in pork chop (not thick-cut)

Salt

Freshly ground black pepper

1 medium shallot, cut into thin rings

1 tablespoon plus 1 teaspoon avocado or other high-heat oil, plus more for shallots

2 garlic cloves, thinly sliced

2 or 3 stalks Swiss chard, stems thinly sliced, leaves torn

¼ cup chicken stock or broth

¼ cup cooked, canned white or cannellini beans, drained

1 to 2 tablespoons cold unsalted butter, cubed

1 teaspoon apple cider vinegar

1. Pat the pork dry with paper towels. Season both sides liberally with salt and pepper. Set aside.

2. Toss the shallot lightly with oil in a microwave-safe bowl. Cook on high, stirring every 30 seconds, until light golden brown, 2 minutes. Transfer them to a paper towel–lined plate to drain.

3. Heat 1 tablespoon of oil in a cast-iron skillet over medium-high heat until it is shimmering. Add the chop and cook it until it is brown and cooked through, 3 minutes per side, or until the internal temperature reaches 135°F (temperature will rise another 10 degrees while resting). Transfer it to a serving plate.

4. Reduce the heat to medium and add the remaining 1 teaspoon of oil. Add the garlic and Swiss chard stems, cooking them until they are soft and fragrant, 2 minutes.

5. Add the stock and scrape up the browned bits. Add the beans and bring to a simmer. Cook until the liquid has evaporated and the beans are tender, 3 minutes. Add the greens in the last minute or so of cooking to wilt them.

6. Remove the skillet from the heat and allow it to cool slightly. Using tongs, top the pork chop with the greens. Add the butter, 1 cube at a time, to the skillet, stirring until melted and creamy. Spoon the mixture around the pork. Season with pepper and splash the vinegar over all. Top the pork with the crispy shallots and enjoy.

LEMON CHICKEN WITH PEAS AND POTATOES

PREP TIME: 10 MINUTES / COOK TIME: 20 MINUTES

Inspired by classic chicken Vesuvio, this dish combines skin-on chicken (boneless cooks faster) for extra juiciness with peas, potatoes, and plenty of lemon and garlic. I added spinach for a little extra green, or you could use whatever leftover greens you might have on hand.

1 boneless, skin-on chicken breast

Salt

Freshly ground black pepper

2 tablespoons extra-virgin olive oil

2 red potatoes or 3 or 4 fingerling potatoes, cut into small wedges

2 garlic cloves, minced

½ teaspoon dried oregano

¼ cup chicken broth or stock

Juice from 1 lemon

⅓ cup fresh or frozen peas

1 big handful baby spinach leaves

1. Place a cast-iron skillet in the oven and preheat to 375°F.
2. Season the chicken liberally with salt and pepper.
3. When the skillet is hot, use oven mitts to transfer it to the stovetop. Pour in the olive oil and give the skillet a swirl to coat it.
4. Heat the skillet over medium heat. Add the chicken, skin-side down, and the potatoes and cook until they are brown, flipping halfway through, 8 minutes. Add the garlic and cook until fragrant, 30 seconds.
5. Turn off the heat. Sprinkle the chicken and potatoes with oregano. Pour the stock and lemon juice into the skillet.
6. Return the skillet to the oven and bake until the potatoes are cooked through, the liquid has mostly evaporated, and the internal temperature of the chicken reads 155°F to 160°F (temperature will rise about 10 degrees while resting). Transfer the chicken and potatoes to a plate and let rest at least 5 minutes.
7. Add the peas and spinach to the skillet, turning with tongs until warmed and wilted. Transfer the spinach to the plate. Pour the skillet juices and peas over it and enjoy.

LAMB KEBOBS WITH MINT RAITA

PREP TIME: 10 MINUTES / COOK TIME: 15 MINUTES

Kofta, often made with ground lamb, is the inspiration for this flavorful, spice-forward dish made refreshing with mint-yogurt sauce. Serve with leftover naan and cucumber-tomato-feta salad (see page 66), or stuff kebobs into a pita with the sauce and some lettuce and cucumber.

FOR THE MINT RAITA

⅓ cup yogurt

¼ cup packed fresh mint leaves, chopped

Zest and juice of ½ lemon

FOR THE KEBOBS

4 to 6 ounces ground lamb

1 tablespoon chopped fresh parsley (optional)

1 tablespoon chopped fresh mint

1 small shallot, minced (or ¼ teaspoon onion powder)

1 garlic clove, minced (or ¼ teaspoon garlic powder)

¼ teaspoon ground cumin

¼ teaspoon ground coriander

¼ teaspoon ground sumac or salt

¼ teaspoon freshly ground black pepper

⅛ teaspoon ground cinnamon

TO MAKE THE MINT RAITA

1. Preheat the oven to 450°F and combine the yogurt, mint, zest, and lemon juice in a small bowl and refrigerate until ready to serve.

TO MAKE THE KEBOBS

2. Combine the lamb, parsley (if using), mint, shallot, garlic, cumin, coriander, sumac, pepper, and cinnamon in a medium bowl and gently mix with clean hands. Shape the mixture into 3 cigar-shaped kebobs, about 4 inches long. Thread each kebob onto a skewer, flattening a bit with the palm of your hand.

3. Place the kebobs on a rimmed baking sheet and bake until they are golden brown and the internal temperature reads 165°F, 15 minutes. You can also sear them on a hot grill pan over medium heat, flipping occasionally, until cooked through, 6 to 8 minutes.

4. Transfer the kebobs to a serving plate. Serve with the mint raita and enjoy.

Ingredient Tip: Visit the butcher counter for a smaller portion of ground lamb, or they might even be able to grind lamb meat fresh for you. You can always substitute ground beef if you have trouble finding ground lamb.

Make It Faster: If you can find it, purchase a Ras al Hanout spice blend and use about a tablespoon to flavor the kebobs instead of other spices. You can also simply form the kebobs into round balls and skip the skewers.

TURKEY AND ROASTED RED PEPPER MEATBALLS

GOOD FOR SCALING / PREP TIME: 15 MINUTES / COOK TIME: 15 MINUTES

Ground turkey can be bland and boring, but these meatballs—thanks to the red pepper and plenty of herbs and spices—are super tasty and tender, too. This recipe makes enough for this dish and for Turkey Meatball Soup with Swiss Chard and Dill (page 51), but you could double it to use all the ground turkey and freeze meatballs for later use.

½ jar store-bought marinara or 1 (14.5-ounce) can tomato sauce

½ pound ground turkey

4 jarred roasted red peppers, drained, finely chopped (about ¼ cup)

1 piece bread, torn Into very small pieces, or ¼ cup panko bread crumbs

1 tablespoon chopped fresh parsley

½ tablespoon garlic powder

½ tablespoon onion powder

¼ teaspoon salt

¼ teaspoon freshly ground black pepper

1 large egg

Basil leaves, torn

Grated Parmesan cheese, for garnish

1. Heat the marinara in a 4-quart pot or deep skillet over medium heat, while making the meatballs.
2. Combine the turkey, peppers, bread, parsley, garlic powder, onion powder, salt, and pepper in a large bowl. Crack the egg into the bowl and gently mix it to combine, without overmixing. Shape the mixture into eight 2-inch balls, slightly larger than a golf ball, dropping four of them, one by one, into the sauce.
3. Turn the meatballs gently with a spoon to coat them with the sauce. Cover and simmer until cooked through (or internal temperature reaches 165°F), 15 minutes. Serve over your favorite cooked pasta, spaghetti squash, or just a bed of spinach. Garnish with basil and Parmesan.

Preparation Tip: Add more vegetables to this dish by adding diced zucchini to the sauce while simmering the meatballs. You could also add 2 ounces of pasta to the sauce while simmering for a one-pot option, but add more sauce or ¼ cup water to the pot at the beginning of cooking time.

BUTTER CHICKEN WITH CILANTRO

PREP TIME: 10 MINUTES / COOK TIME: 20 MINUTES

Once I discovered butter chicken, my life changed—in a good way. This is a quicker-cooking version of the Indian dish, but if you have the time, you can marinate the chicken for a few hours or even overnight to infuse flavors and tenderize. It's traditional to enjoy butter chicken over rice, but you could always use some cauliflower rice instead for an extra vegetable (see the tip).

½ cup sour cream (or Greek yogurt)

1 tablespoon lemon juice

½ tablespoon turmeric

½ tablespoon garam masala

2 teaspoons ground cumin, divided

2 or 3 boneless, skinless chicken thighs, cut into 1-inch pieces

2 tablespoons unsalted butter

½ cup chopped onion

2 garlic cloves, minced

¼ teaspoon ground ginger

¼ teaspoon ground cinnamon

¼ teaspoon salt

¼ teaspoon freshly ground black pepper

1 cup canned tomato sauce (pureed tomatoes)

¼ cup full-fat coconut milk

Chopped fresh cilantro, for garnish

1. Mix together the sour cream, lemon juice, turmeric, garam masala, and 1½ teaspoons cumin in a medium bowl. Add the chicken and stir to completely coat. Cover the bowl and refrigerate.

2. Melt the butter in a medium skillet over medium heat. Add the onion and cook until lightly caramelized, 3 minutes, stirring occasionally. Add the garlic, the remaining ½ teaspoon cumin, ginger, cinnamon, salt, and pepper and cook until fragrant, 1 more minute.

3. Stir in the tomato sauce, chicken, and coconut milk. Cover the skillet and bring to a simmer. Cook, uncovered, until the chicken is cooked through, stirring occasionally, 12 to 15 minutes.

4. Serve with cooked rice or cauliflower rice, and garnish with cilantro.

Preparation Tip: To easily make cauliflower rice, microwave 1 cup of chopped cauliflower florets and 1 tablespoon coconut oil at 50 percent power for 4 to 5 minutes, stirring occasionally, while you cook the chicken. Check the freezer aisle of your grocery store—more places now offer bagged, prechopped frozen cauliflower rice that works perfectly for this quick-cooking method.

CHAPTER 8

Desserts

< Chocolate Chip Chickpea Blondies,
  page 117

CHOCOLATE–ALMOND BUTTER DATES

PREP TIME: 10 MINUTES, PLUS 20 MINUTES REFRIGERATION TIME

Who needs sugary candy when you can make a way healthier (and still tasty) treat? These guilt-free nuggets store well in the freezer for when you want a small bite of something sweet that won't wreck your day (or night).

¼ cup almond or peanut butter

½ teaspoon pure vanilla extract

⅛ teaspoon ground cinnamon

10 Medjool dates, pitted

½ cup chopped dark chocolate or chocolate chips

8 ounces dark chocolate, chopped

1 tablespoon coconut oil

1. Combine the almond butter, vanilla, and cinnamon in a small bowl. Mash with a fork until combined and smooth.

2. Moisten your fingertips to prevent sticking. Stuff each date with about a teaspoon of the nut butter mixture.

3. Microwave the chocolate and oil in a microwave-safe bowl on 40 percent power, stirring once or twice, until melted and shiny, 2 minutes.

4. Using a fork, dunk the dates, one by one, into the chocolate and transfer them to a plate. Refrigerate the dates until they are firm, at least 20 minutes. To freeze, place the plate in the freezer and transfer the dates to a resealable plastic bag once frozen.

Preparation Tip: If you just want to make a few dates at a time and want the chocolate taste without the whole dunking process, you can microwave the nut butter mixture with a little chocolate and coconut oil and stuff that into each date.

LEMON-GINGER "COOKIE" BITES

PREP TIME: 10 MINUTES, PLUS 15 MINUTES FREEZER TIME

These little bites of joy are so pleasantly refreshing after a meal, or even as an afternoon pick-me-up without that sugar rush and crash that traditional cookies cause. Made with naturally sweet dates, which are rich in potassium, and combined with protein-rich nuts and nut butter that also have healthy fats, they can be enjoyed as a nutritious snack or dessert.

12 pitted Medjool dates

1 cup unsalted, dry roasted or raw cashews

2 tablespoons almond butter

Zest and juice of 1 lemon

½ teaspoon ground ginger

¼ teaspoon turmeric (optional)

¼ teaspoon ground cinnamon

⅛ teaspoon pure vanilla extract

Pinch salt

Unsweetened coconut flakes, for rolling (optional)

1. Place the dates in a food processor and pulse a few times to chop them. Add the cashews, almond butter, zest, lemon juice, ginger, turmeric (if using), cinnamon, vanilla, and salt, and process until a sticky "dough" forms.

2. Shape the dough into golf ball–size balls. Roll each one in coconut flakes (if using). Place each ball on a plate or small baking sheet and place in the freezer to firm up, at least 15 minutes.

Tip: To store the bites for up to 3 months, leave them in the freezer. When they are frozen, transfer them to a resealable plastic bag.

STRAWBERRY "ICE CREAM"

**IN A PINCH / PREP TIME: 5 MINUTES, PLUS 5 MINUTES BLENDING TIME /
MAKES ABOUT 2 LARGE SCOOPS**

Craving ice cream but don't want all the extra sugar? Use frozen fruit instead! This is an easy, quick recipe for an indulgent but healthy treat. Using a food processor helps break down the frozen fruit. If you only have a blender, work in small batches to puree the strawberries completely.

1 can full-fat coconut milk (refrigerated overnight)

2 cups frozen strawberries

½ cup plain Greek yogurt

1 tablespoon maple syrup or honey (optional)

Chocolate chips (optional)

1. Scoop out the coconut solids from the can of coconut milk into the bowl of a food processor. Refrigerate the remaining coconut milk for later use.

2. Add the strawberries, yogurt, and maple syrup (if using). Process until smooth, 2 minutes.

3. Scoop the mixture into a bowl. Top with chocolate chips (if using) and enjoy.

CHOCOLATE CHIP CHICKPEA BLONDIES

PREP TIME: 5 MINUTES / COOK TIME: 25 MINUTES

I'm seriously obsessed with these gluten-free treats because (a) they taste like chocolate chip cookies but without the sugar or flour, and (b) you can whip them up in seconds using a food processor. You kind of need to make the whole batch for the blondies to bake properly, but they freeze well for dessert on the fly.

1 (15-ounce) can chickpeas, drained, rinsed

½ cup peanut or almond butter

⅓ cup maple syrup

1 teaspoon pure vanilla extract

¼ teaspoon baking soda

¼ teaspoon baking powder

⅛ teaspoon salt

⅓ cup chocolate chips or more, if wanted

3 tablespoons coarsely chopped walnuts or pecans (optional)

1. Preheat the oven to 350°F. Grease an 8-by-8-inch baking pan.

2. Combine the chickpeas, peanut butter, maple syrup, vanilla, baking soda, baking powder, and salt in a food processor. Pulse until smooth, scraping down the sides once or twice. Fold in the chocolate chips and nuts (if using).

3. Pour the mixture into the prepared pan, spreading it smooth with a spatula. Bake until a toothpick or knife inserted in the center comes out clean, 20 to 25 minutes. Cool the pan on a wire rack.

4. Cut the blondies into 2-by-2-inch squares.

Tip: Cool the blondies completely, about 20 minutes, before freezing them. To freeze, place the blondies on a baking sheet and place in the freezer. When they're frozen, transfer to a resealable plastic bag.

BAKED CINNAMON-APPLE CRISP

PREP TIME: 5 MINUTES / COOK TIME: 25 MINUTES

Whenever I find myself with leftover apple (or pear) slices, I make this crisp for dessert. Oats and nuts replace the flour in a traditional crisp for a more nutritious version.

1 apple, peeled, cored, and diced

1 teaspoon lemon juice

½ teaspoon ground cinnamon

¼ cup oats

2 tablespoons chopped, unsalted nuts

1 tablespoon maple syrup or honey

2 tablespoons cold butter, cubed

1. Heat the oven to 350°F.

2. Place the diced apples in a 6-ounce (3.5-inch) ramekin. Add the lemon juice and cinnamon, tossing to coat.

3. In a small bowl, whisk together the oats, nuts, and maple syrup with a fork. Add the butter and mash until heavy crumbs form.

4. Spoon the crumb mixture over the apples. Bake until the apples are tender and bubbly, 20 to 25 minutes.

Ingredient Tip: Feel free to substitute sliced pear for the apple slices. Also, any nut or nut mixture works (almonds, walnuts, pecans, hazelnuts, macadamia nuts, etc.).

MAPLE-BANANA BREAD PUDDING

IN A PINCH / PREP TIME: 5 MINUTES / COOK TIME: 15 MINUTES

When that banana has been on your counter too long, it's time to a) freeze it for a smoothie, or b) make this delicious and easy-to-make dessert. Leftover bread also works well in this recipe.

1 teaspoon unsalted butter, at room temperature, plus more for greasing

1 ripe banana

1 large egg

¼ cup low-fat vanilla Greek yogurt

2 teaspoons maple syrup, plus more for serving

1 teaspoon pure vanilla extract

1 slice sourdough or other leftover bread, crusts removed, cubed

2 tablespoons chopped walnuts

1. Preheat the oven to 350°F. Grease a 10-ounce ramekin with the butter.

2. Mash the banana in a large bowl. Add the egg, yogurt, maple syrup, and vanilla, whisking to combine. Fold in the bread.

3. Pour the mixture into the prepared ramekin. Cover with aluminum foil and bake until steaming hot and puffed in the center, 10 minutes.

4. Melt 1 teaspoon of butter in the microwave using a small microwave-safe bowl. Stir in the walnuts and additional maple syrup, if desired. Remove the foil from the ramekin and sprinkle the walnuts over the pudding. Return to the oven to brown, 3 to 5 minutes.

NO-BAKE CHEESECAKE

PREP TIME: 10 MINUTES, PLUS 20 MINUTES FREEZING

Cheesecake is definitely my all-time favorite dessert, but who has time to make it? Plus, I know all the sugar and the graham cracker crust isn't great for me. This no-bake version uses a nut crust (use any and all types of nuts you want) and a lemony filling with just a few ingredients.

1 tablespoon coconut oil or unsalted butter, melted

¼ cup finely chopped nuts (hazelnuts, macadamia nuts, walnuts, etc., or a combination)

⅛ teaspoon ground cinnamon

3 ounces cream cheese, at room temperature

1 tablespoon sweetener of choice

1 teaspoon lemon zest

1. Melt the coconut oil in a small bowl in the microwave. Add the nuts and cinnamon and stir to coat.
2. Press the mixture into the bottom of a 3-ounce ramekin.
3. In another small bowl, whip the cream cheese with the sweetener and lemon zest with a fork. Spoon the filling atop the crust, spreading with a rubber spatula to even out.
4. Place the cheesecake in the freezer to firm up, at least 20 minutes. Serve with fresh berries or berry sauce (see the tip) and enjoy.

Make It Faster: Chop nuts in a food processor until fine, or use almond flour.

Preparation Tip: Top with fresh strawberries, or to make a quick sauce, microwave frozen blueberries or strawberries with a touch of coconut oil for about 90 seconds and mash the mixture with a fork.

MEASUREMENT CONVERSIONS

VOLUME EQUIVALENTS (LIQUID)

US STANDARD	US STANDARD (OUNCES)	METRIC (APPROXIMATE)
2 tablespoons	1 fl. oz.	30 mL
¼ cup	2 fl. oz.	60 mL
½ cup	4 fl. oz.	120 mL
1 cup	8 fl. oz.	240 mL
1½ cups	12 fl. oz.	355 mL
2 cups or 1 pint	16 fl. oz.	475 mL
4 cups or 1 quart	32 fl. oz.	1 L
1 gallon	128 fl. oz.	4 L

VOLUME EQUIVALENTS (DRY)

US STANDARD	METRIC (APPROXIMATE)
⅛ teaspoon	0.5 mL
¼ teaspoon	1 ml
½ teaspoon	2 mL
¾ teaspoon	4 mL
1 teaspoon	5 mL
1 tablespoon	15 mL
¼ cup	59 mL
⅓ cup	79 mL
½ cup	118 mL
⅔ cup	156 mL
¾ cup	177 mL
1 cup	235 mL
2 cups or 1 pint	475 mL
3 cups	700 mL
4 cups or 1 quart	1 L

OVEN TEMPERATURES

FAHRENHEIT	CELSIUS (APPROXIMATE)
250°F	120°C
300°F	150°C
325°F	165°C
350°F	180°C
375°F	190°C
400°F	200°C
425°F	220°C
450°F	230°C

WEIGHT EQUIVALENTS

US STANDARD	METRIC (APPROXIMATE)
½ ounce	15 g
1 ounce	30 g
2 ounces	60 g
4 ounces	115 g
8 ounces	225 g
12 ounces	340 g
16 ounces or 1 pound	455 g

INDEX

ACKNOWLEDGMENTS

In addition to my solo cook friends (a big shout out to you, Danika!) who provided me with a wealth of ideas for this book (as well as my brother, Andrew, and sister-in-law, Nicole), I would also like to thank my number one taste tester and husband, Harvey Henao; my son and taste-tester-in-training, Jonah; and my daughter and expert kitchen assistant, Lily. Also, a big thank-you to my mom, Karen Levin, a cookbook author and 30-minute guru who has taught me over the years how to develop recipes that work and in a tight time frame.

I would also like to thank Gurvinder Gandu, who provided great feedback and kept me on track during the entire process, and Meredith Tennant for her expert recipe editing. Thank you, also, to the entire team at Callisto, who developed the idea for this book, hired me to write it, and worked hard to put it all together.

ABOUT THE AUTHOR

 **Amelia Levin** is an award-winning food writer, B2B magazine editor, former hard news reporter, certified chef, and certified holistic nutritionist who has been writing about food, food service, and chefs for the past fifteen years. She is the author of six cookbooks, including this book and Callisto titles *Paleo for Everyday* and *The Complete Pegan Diet for Beginners*, and she has ghostwritten or contributed to four others. Amelia lives in the Chicago area with her husband, Harvey Henao, and two children, Jonah and Liliana (Lily). Read more about Amelia and her work at AmeliaLevin.com.